Just
Breathe

Just Breathe

A Caregiver's Journey Through
the Depths of Dementia

Mary Kay Verhoff

proving
press

Book Design & Production:
Columbus Publishing Lab
www.ColumbusPublishingLab.com

Paperback ISBN: 978-1-63337-818-6
Ebook ISBN: 978-1-63337-819-3
LCCN: 2024914772

Printed in the United States of America
1 3 5 7 9 10 8 6 4 2

Contents

Preface   i

Prologue   iii

PART ONE: The Beginning   1

    1. The Early Years   3
    2. Is It My Imagination?   7
    3. The Day That Everything Changed   11
    4. The Bumpy Road to a Diagnosis   15
    5. Digging into the Details   21

PART TWO: The Middle Years: Living With Dementia   25

    6. Adjusting to a New Life   27
    7. Perpetual Loss and Grief   31
    8. Finding Humor   37
    9. Strength, Courage and Resilience   43
    10. The Anchors   49
    11. Loss of Relationships   53
    12. The Well-Intended Ones   57
    13. Those Trying Tiring Days   61
    14. Challenging Holidays   65
    15. Creating Good Days   69
    16. Dealing with Anger   73
    17. Gaslighting   77
    18. Recharging   81
    19. A New Attitude   85
    20. Hope   89
    21. Patient or Spouse?   93
    22. Where Did I Go?   99

PART THREE: The Final Chapter   103

    23. End of Care Choices   105
    24. Adjusting to Placement   111
    25. The Beginning of the End   115
    26. Dying Is a Process   121

Epilogue   125

Acknowledgments   129

Preface

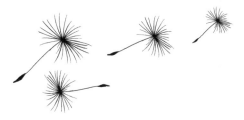

THROUGHOUT THE JOURNEY OF MY HUSBAND'S DEMENTIA, the image of a dandelion has always popped into my mind.

Dementia begins to slowly show up like a dandelion. You can deny the subtle signs and try to ignore them as occasional quirks. But the weed gets taller and stronger, and suddenly it's in full bloom and you're no longer able to explain it away.

As the life cycle of the disease progresses, bit by bit the seeds die off and begin to leave the vibrant flower. Occasionally, the winds blow and hasten the process until, eventually, the entire flower is gone.

The unknowns and fear cause much anxiety, even panic, and you need to remind yourself to just breathe. The petals will continue to wither and fall, but as caregivers, we do the best we can to minimize or slow the losses one step, one breath at a time.

Looking at a field of dandelions, they all look the same, but each is actually unique, and bees will draw from particular ones just what they need. Each person with dementia is unique, even though they may have similarities. Each caregiver, too, has his or her own individual personality. We need to acknowledge that there will ii • Just Breathe

never be instructions in a one-size-fits-all format, or a Caregiving for Dummies manual. Each path is extraordinary and each caregiver soon learns to focus on this day, sometimes this minute.

We could learn a lot from a dandelion. What we see depends a lot on what we are looking for. If I went back to the beginning of Dan's illness, I would see all the weeds in my path and how everything we had dreamed of and planned for was going to fall apart. Yes, a lot of that happened, and more. But I did things that I didn't know I was capable of doing. I learned who the most important people are in my life. They are the ones who stood beside us and tried, in their own way, to comfort us and ease our pain.

Like a dandelion, life is always a balance of hanging on and letting go. Caring for someone with dementia is an awful lot of letting go, but it's also a blessing to find and hold on to those people who help you wade through the weeds and plant seeds of hope for the future.

This is our story. I can't tell you how many times I caught myself holding my breath, especially in the beginning, or when experiencing yet another loss. You learn to adjust to the new normal, which continually changes. There's no cure. Not yet. There's no magical potion to apply before all the seeds of the dandelion blow away. Remember, you are strong enough to handle anything. Just Breathe!

Prologue

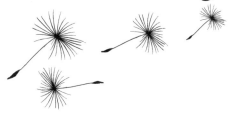

CAREGIVING FOR A SPOUSE WITH DEMENTIA is probably one of the toughest jobs you'll ever experience. It's not for sissies. I wish I was a sissy sometimes. I wish I wasn't so strong-willed. Maybe, if I had been a sissy, dementia wouldn't have chosen our family.

I've always been a take-charge kind of person, grabbing new challenges with both hands and standing up for what I believe is right. I've also been someone with little tolerance and patience. Dementia sure laughed at me! It kicked the door down and said, "I'm here. Deal with me!"

From that point on, it was boss. Not me. It didn't care about my 30 years of management experience in a health-care setting. We were just along for the ride with every twisting and turning descent.

Our journey was 10 years of fear, loss after loss, frustration, anger, guilt, renewed love and laughter. Yes, even laughter. All the feels. We traveled a winding road of strength, weakness, perseverance, defeat and love. Much love.

I'm so thankful that I journaled throughout much of Dan's illness. When spoken words failed, this is where my thoughts and raw emotions flowed. This release helped me rest at night.

My hope is that our story will help you as a caregiver to realize that whatever you feel in that moment is ok. There is no normal with dementia, but whatever you feel is normal for you. You are handling a very abnormal and unchartered situation with as much normalcy as you can. Each difficult moment will pass. Maybe like a kidney stone, but it will pass and give you the strength and courage to face the next.

PART ONE

The
Beginning

CHAPTER 1
The Early Years

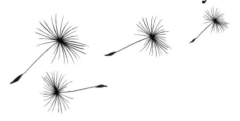

OUR STORY BEGAN like so many other couples. We were young, naïve, in love, and both grew up and lived in the same small rural town in northwest Ohio. I was a senior in high school and Dan was two years older. We were set up by mutual friends and our first date was on a hay ride, sponsored by the local Jaycee Club. That actual date was ok, but mainly because I was with my other friends. I didn't have a particularly good time, if truth be told. But then he dropped me off at my front door, and I quickly found out that he was a spectacular kisser and agreed to a second date that turned into a third.

It wasn't long before I knew that I was falling for this tall, funny, strong young man, who was prematurely turning bald at only age 19. Other than my own dad, I'd never seen such a hard-working man who could fix or build just about anything. I knew he was the one.

After two years of dating, we were married in 1977 in our local Catholic Church on a day filled with torrential rains. The whole time I was getting ready and listening to the thunder and the downpour outside, I was being told that it was good luck to get married on a rainy day. (I still think they made that up!) But it was a beautiful ceremony, followed by a joyous reception and a honeymoon up to Sault Ste. Marie, Canada.

As I was still finishing my college degree in medical imaging and not yet working, we started off our marriage on a pretty rocky financial ground, relying on only his salary at a manufacturing plant. But somehow, we survived. I was a decent cook, he wasn't picky, and we both learned to live on big cheap casseroles that we ate for days.

After I graduated from college and started working, we were able to make ends meet without counting every single penny. Before long, we purchased a home and started a family. First came our daughter, Kelly, in 1980. We were over the moon at being parents, and she was pretty easy on us since we were new at the parenting thing. Then in 1983, our second daughter, Becky, arrived, three weeks late, but she finally decided to make her appearance. She showed up telling us that we'd better buckle up. She was colicky, didn't sleep well, and had frequent bouts of projectile vomiting. As a 3-year-old with no filter, Kelly asked us when we were going to take her back.

But then life just went on in a typical fashion. The girls went to school and grew up fast. My role in my job at the hospital grew as well, and Dan stayed solid at the manufacturing plant, making farm equipment. We had the normal ups and downs that all families go through - minor health issues, financial hiccups, family drama, emotional baggage, but also lots of fun and laughter. Through it all, even in the roughest of times, we remained committed to our marriage vows.

Dan always had a passion for fishing, specifically bass fishing. He belonged to several bass clubs during our marriage, and

I used to tell him that he loved fishing more than me. Then he would tell me that I was still #1 in the off-season. He had two bass boats, one for larger lakes and one for smaller lakes and ponds. People would ask him why he had two and he would say, "Because my wife won't let me have three."

Seriously, his obsession was often annoying. If he wasn't fishing, he was watching bass tournaments on TV, looking through bass magazines or tinkering with his boats. But I always knew that I just needed to tell him that dinner was ready, and he would come running with a big appetite and an endless grin.

I always knew how much he loved me. Not only did he tell me frequently, but his actions showed it. If I had a long, hard day at work, he would have dinner ready. We knew it would either be fried eggs or French toast because those seemed to be the only recipes he knew. But it was still greatly appreciated. Now and then he would shake things up by throwing chocolate syrup into the batter. He didn't shy away from doing dishes and I fondly remember catching him running the sweeper in his bathrobe and a cowboy hat.

He had a big heart and loved making me smile. Oh, he could be critical, and I knew how to push his buttons, which caused quite a bit of discord, but we never had to wonder how much we were loved.

When the girls were nearly adults, Dan and I bought a camper and found an ideal spot on a lake about two hours from our home. We loved it there. It was our happy place. We bought a pontoon and suddenly we were a three-boat family after all, much to my chagrin. Our goal was to retire and spend our summers there and travel to a warmer climate in the winter. We made a whole new family of friends in our campground and upgraded our camper a few times, which I appreciated because I figured out that I really don't like camping. I like glamping. I need my air conditioning, satellite TV and all the comforts of home.

After Kelly finished college, she began her teaching career and got married. She and Jeromie brought great joy to our lives when their children, Lauren and Levi, were born. Dan and I were further overjoyed when Becky and her husband, Jason, were married and blessed us with the births of grandsons Maddox and Sebastian. We also welcomed Jason's daughter, Kaya, into our growing family.

We spent as much time as possible with our daughters and their beautiful families. Everything seemed perfect. After 35 years of marriage, we were literally cruising along in a bass boat or on a pontoon when our plans began to capsize.

CHAPTER 2

Is It My Imagination?

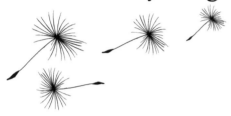

I CAN'T SAY that there was a specific date or event that I can pin-point and say, "Ah, there it is. That's where it started." That first year of our 10-year struggle with dementia was marked by my occasional feelings of wanting to say, "Dan, you aren't paying attention," or "How could you forget that?" or "We just had this discussion!"

I thought he was just overworked and tired. He had been working a lot of overtime while I had a very stressful management job and was probably short on patience. Sometimes I felt that he was gaslighting me. We would have a discussion about something, then a few minutes later it was as if it never occurred. He would swear that I imagined it. Maybe I did. Maybe the discussion had been all in my head.

These episodes seemed to increase and there were instances when he wouldn't remember how to do a simple task. I made a concerted effort to let him get a good nap in after work, then a hearty dinner, and try not to stress him out.

But for the most part, that first year was normal, with just an occasional quirky moment, a moment that made me pause and feel an unsettling pit in my stomach.

Year two came and we were busy getting ready for Becky's wedding. Again, I brushed off the short-term memory episodes with the stress of the wedding planning, our work schedules and fitting in all of his bass tournament details.

In that second year, we made a day trip up to Lake Erie to visit some friends and do some sightseeing. We had a long conversation about a trip we would be taking in the fall, and about 20 minutes later, he had no recollection of that discussion. Then a very similar thing happened a month later when we were on our way to set up for Becky's wedding. At the service and reception, he seemed very nervous, unable to focus and was unusually emotional. Again, I shrugged it off as stress.

A month later, we took that fall trip to San Francisco, Napa Valley and Sonoma. It was a much- needed getaway for both of us, and probably the most time we had spent together, just the two of us, in a very long time. It also was a lot of together time to notice more idiosyncrasies. On one particular morning, we stood outside of a restaurant looking at the map of the piers and pointing out places we wanted to visit. Then we went inside, ordered our breakfast and sat down at a table near the window, which had a view of the map outside that we had just studied.

He said, "We need to find a map so that you can find the places that you want to visit."

I felt my stomach turn over and just knew something wasn't right. That is one instance that I can definitely say was a defining moment.

We had an amazing trip and I will always cherish it, but from that time forward, I just knew that there was a storm brewing. I distinctly remember waiting on our connecting flight coming home at the Dallas airport, when he told me he had to use the restroom and took off down the corridor. I sat on pins and needles waiting and wondering if he would be able to find his way back. But he did, and I felt myself take a deep, relaxing breath.

These little oddities continued and grew in frequency. At one point, as we were driving to our camper one Friday after work, I noticed that he would turn his signal on when passing cars on the freeway but never turned it off. Not a big deal, but after telling him about it for the hundredth time, I asked him with much trepidation, "Are you having trouble doing your job at work?"

I had been nervously holding that thought for over a year and a half and suddenly, I just blurted it out. He kept reassuring me that everything was fine and there were no work issues. But the waters were getting murkier and I couldn't stop the raging flood ahead.

At one point, Dan was seeing his family physician for a weird rash that wouldn't go away, and I boldly called that doctor and said I wanted a referral to a dermatologist and that, hey, while I have you on the phone, I'm worried about his short-term memory and executive functioning. This refers to a person's ability to plan, organize, manage time, remember details, and be able to multi task. It's generally controlled by the frontal lobe of the brain.

I told his doctor that Dan was losing things, had little awareness of time, spatial problems when parking his van, and seemed to struggle with searching for the right words. The doctor dismissed it and replied that he hadn't noticed anything but would make the dermatology referral for the rash. Long story short on that issue is that he ended up having a biopsy and was diagnosed with a rare autoimmune disease called dermatomyositis. We were referred to a rheumatology doctor and Dan started on a weekly shot of Methotrexate until a few months before he passed.

I was also able to get him into a doctor who specialized in functional medicine. A lot of labs were completed and it was found that he had an extremely low Vitamin D level and several other results that were off the charts, including low hemoglobin. This doctor put him on a strict gluten free and noninflammatory diet, along with many supplements. His energy level improved, but the memory and executive function issues still lingered, and I started journaling to keep all the complex appointments, emotions and worries in check. Life went on, as did my growing fear that something was horribly wrong.

CHAPTER 3

The Day That Everything Changed

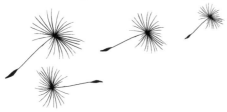

I WILL NEVER FORGET the details of the day that everything changed. I remember the outfit I was wearing at work. I remember the project I was working on in my office. I remember the time was 1:15.

My cell phone rang and I answered it, hoping that the intrusion wouldn't take long because I needed to get back to my project. But on the other end of the line was the owner of the manufacturing plant where Dan worked. As soon as he said hello, I knew. I just knew.

I held my breath and waited for the news that I had been dreading.

"Mary, we need to talk. About Dan."

Without any other information, I said, "Steve, I knew this call would come someday."

He went on to describe that Dan had been struggling at work for a while, but his coworkers had been covering for him and giving him easier jobs which they thought he could handle. On this particular day, they found him standing in the parking lot after his lunch break and staring at the stones. They got him back to work but knew something had to be done. It was too dangerous for him to be welding, grinding and operating a tow motor. Steve said they could no longer allow him to work for his own safety as well as those around him, until he underwent testing and a physician deemed it safe for him to return. He kindly asked if he should tell him or allow me to give him the news. I replied that I would do it. I didn't want him driving home with that added stress.

I sat paralyzed with fear for several minutes. I had haunting flashbacks of his mom who died of Alzheimer's and his sister who had it at that time, too. They were in their late seventies and early eighties when diagnosed. Dan was only 58. It couldn't be that!

I made an urgent dash to my boss's office and asked to see her right away. By the time she called me back to her room, I was near tears and hysteria. After describing what had been going on and the call I had just received, she took over. Working at a large health-care organization does have its advantages. She called the head of our medical staff and asked for guidance. He suggested a family physician in my home county who was fellowship trained in geriatric care and brain issues. We were able to get an appointment for the next day.

Driving home from work (early) that day, I called his sister, Judy. I described what had been going on, the call I had received, and that I was so afraid as to how I was going to tell him that he couldn't go back to work, something that was a huge part of his identity. She met me at our home, and we sat and waited for him to arrive. When he walked in and saw us both sitting there, I'm sure he was wondering why I was home earlier than normal and what the two of us were conspiring together.

I sat him down and just came straight out with the call I had gotten from Steve. His first response was, "Oh, it'll be all right. I'll talk to him about it when I go to work tomorrow."

Judy said, "Dan, you're not understanding. You're not allowed to go back to work until we figure out what's going on with you."

I told him we had an appointment the next day, and hopefully we'd get some answers. But all he kept saying was, "Everything's ok. I was just tired today." He was very dismissive of it all. Nothing more was said that evening, and I went to bed filled with so much fear and dread.

> … *Dear Journal, this is my first entry. Today I received a call from Dan's boss. The other shoe has dropped. All my worry has been warranted. My gut tells me that Dan has dementia, but I can't say that word out loud. I feel like I can't breathe. I feel like the walls are caving in and swallowing me up. Dear Heavenly Father, give me the strength and courage to face whatever is ahead of us.*

CHAPTER 4

The Bumpy Road to a Diagnosis

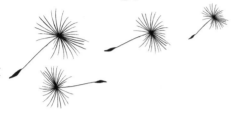

WALKING INTO THAT PHYSICIAN'S OFFICE was one of the scariest moments of my life. She was the kindest physician I had ever met. When she saw the fear in my eyes, she kept things lighthearted and made small talk, as she did a thorough exam of Dan and administered a mental test. She laughed when she discovered that he had the wherewithal to actually cheat on one of the tasks.

Although there were signs of dementia and he had a borderline score, she said it could also be anxiety disorder. She ordered anxiety medication and a barrage of tests, including a CT scan of the brain, bloodwork, and a sleep study. All of the results were essentially normal. She suggested that we try the anxiety meds for a few months to see if they made a difference. They did not. Although he appeared much calmer and less stressed on the meds, he continued to struggle with short-term memory and thought processes.

Over the next year and a half, we tried SO many things. The doctor was very sympathetic and understanding. I refused to give up and kept researching and wanting to try literally everything. For example, he saw a chiropractor who did muscle testing. He told Dan that he had high levels of iron in his system and gave him supplements to take. We did that religiously but to no avail.

We next traveled to a neurologist in Columbus, Ohio, who put him through a variety of mental tests. Becky went with us to that appointment, and I had told them both not to add that his mom and sister had Alzheimer's because I was afraid if that was mentioned, the doctor would automatically jump to the same diagnosis. Before any tests were administered, however, Dan told her that his mom and sister had Alzheimer's. I wanted to throttle him.

We left with a diagnosis of early onset Alzheimer's. I cried myself to sleep that night, but I awoke the next day with new resolve. I did not believe her diagnosis. The more I read about it, the more it didn't fit. He had recently started to demonstrate difficulty in finding the words he wanted to say. Yet, he knew people, their names, and could tell stories that even I didn't remember. What was especially troubling was that his executive functioning seemed to be getting worse. On one occasion, he called me out to his garage to help him put oil into the lawn mower because he couldn't remember how to do it.

As a result, I made an appointment with another neurologist about a half hour from our home. He diagnosed Dan with Semantic Dementia. This type of dementia involves language problems. More specifically, the meanings of words are confused and interchanged. That didn't seem to fit either, but at this point I was ready to accept that he did indeed have some type of dementia.

After another appointment with his physician and venting my frustration, she suggested having him see a neuropsychologist and have extensive testing completed. We had to wait several months for the appointment. In the meantime, he had a brain

MRI, which was read as normal. Dan went through four hours of mental testing with the neuropsychologist and we received the results at the completion. He said everything in his testing pointed to severe right hemisphere brain damage. He asked if we were sure that there had never been a brain injury. When we said that there had been none, the doctor didn't know how he was functioning as well as he was. That appointment left me more confused, and I was even more determined to find an answer.

His original doctor then suggested that she refer him to a neurologist at the Cleveland Clinic. After waiting for many months for that appointment, we made the three-hour drive, along with Kelly. At the beginning of the visit, they gave him three words to remember, and all I could think was, "He will never remember these."

Then they poked and prodded, gave him physical and mental tests, and left the room to discuss it. When they came back in, they said we were in the wrong neurology department. This one was for physical issues, not mental. They ordered a new MRI and made an appointment with a physician in the brain division of neurology. Before they left the room, Dan said, "Hey, you forgot to ask me those three words."

The doctor laughed and asked, "Do you remember them?"

Dan proceeded to rattle them off. I had no idea if they were even correct because I had forgotten them, as it had been almost an hour and a half since they were given to him. He was absolutely correct and was quite proud of himself.

We waited another four long months for that next appointment, and Dan and I returned to the Cleveland Clinic, this time by ourselves. The physician was so very conscientious. I sat in the waiting room while they put him through extensive mental testing. After reviewing those test results, comparing his MRI's that were now one-and-a-half years apart, along with the neuropsychologist's evaluation, the doctor sat us down and gave us the diagnosis of Frontotemporal Dementia (FTD) with aphasia. He showed us the MRI comparisons and even though both were read as normal, there was noted shrinkage of his frontal and occipital lobes. He gave us a lot of literature to take home and read, digest and become more educated about how dim the future would be.

Neither of us said a word as we left. I pulled out of the campus and headed down the highway, still numb with the diagnosis. But this time I knew it was true. We stopped to get a bite to eat and Dan very nonchalantly said to me, "There, honey. See? Everything's going to be ok, right? You finally have an answer."

He proceeded to take a big bite out of his cheeseburger and grinned. He was smiling on the outside, while I was screaming on the inside.

> ... *Finally, a diagnosis I can wrap my brain around and agree with. I'm done chasing an answer. I want to cry. No, I want to scream. But I won't. It's been a long bumpy road to get to this diagnosis, but now that we're here, does it really matter what we call it? The death sentence is still the same. Our hopes and dreams, our careful planning and saving for our future together, just went to hell. I can feel the panic rising within me, and there's not a damn thing I can do about this damn disease. FTD. FTD. I always thought that was a florist thing. I want my husband back.*

I don't want FTD in our lives. Where do we go from here? How do we adjust our life together? How long will we even be together? Damn you, FTD!

All caregivers have that experience of getting to the WHAT. What is wrong with my loved one? There's something amiss, but I can't put my finger on what it is. We doctor hop and go through test after test. Months, sometimes years pass, trying to chase the WHAT.

Once you get to the WHAT – the diagnosis, the fear, grief, and anger set in, and you start chasing the WHY. Why did he get this horrific, fatal disease? Is it hereditary? Did he have a head injury? Is it from his work environment? Is it due to diet? Didn't I feed him the right foods?

… For years I chased the WHAT and now I find myself researching the WHY. But I think it's time to pack the WHY away in a closet, not totally forgotten, but less important, because now I'm busy dealing with the HOW. The thought that keeps running through my mind is HOW do we go on with daily living knowing that this fatal disease is lurking over us with so many unknowns ahead? At this point, the WHY won't change anything, especially the trajectory of the problem. This is our new reality. I still have moments of self-pity but I don't dwell there. We both still have living to do. Together.

CHAPTER 5

Digging into the Details

WHEN DAN WAS FIRST TAKEN OFF WORK, he was on short-term disability for six months, so we had that steady income. After that, his long-term disability kicked in for the next six months and we still received a partial income and full health-care insurance. But it became clear long before all was exhausted that he wouldn't be going back to work. Ever. That ship had sailed. It was time to start the ball rolling for permanent disability and get him on Medicare and Social Security Disability.

Whoever said that there was such a thing as the Paper Reduction Act must have been joking. I'm so glad I started the process early and had his doctor to provide every piece of documentation I needed. I had heard so many horror stories of denial after denial and having to get an attorney to get disability approved. I was prepared for a long battle ahead.

I made sure I had every test he ever had done, every date of every appointment and the subsequent diagnosis. I filled out the application on-line, hit SUBMIT and waited. I was prepared to wait months, maybe a year to get him approved. Two weeks after submitting the application, I received a call to say that there would be a phone interview with us in a week. That call came and a very polite gentleman talked with me at length, then Dan, then back to me. He said that Dan would most likely be approved.

About two weeks later, we received the approval letter. He also received Social Security back pay. The whole process was less than six weeks. I know that we are extremely fortunate it all went so well, as many have not had that experience. However, I also know that I was his best advocate and worked hard to make sure that everything possible was included in that application.

After he was put on Medicare, I made an appointment with a health-insurance consultant and found him an advantage plan to supplement his Medicare. I also met with our financial advisor to make sure that all of our investments were in order with appropriate Transfers on Death.

In the middle of all this, we met with an elder law attorney to get all of our assets protected. I can't stress this step enough. Do it as early as possible. There is a five year look back once the trust or LLC is in place. We chose to do an LLC with our daughters as controlling members. Our house had to be appraised and put into the LLC. We had our wills updated and established Powers of Attorney, and Advanced Directives. I felt much relief when that was done, even knowing why we were doing it. Dan went through the motions of signing all the forms, but when it was all over, he just smiled and asked, "Do you feel better now that that's all done?" From there, he started talking about our lawn and the crabgrass.

All of these details seem monotonous and never-ending, but they are so very important to protect the surviving spouse. Each elder law attorney has his or her own preference on how to set up a trust or LLC, but the important thing is to just do it! I can honestly say that the completion of all those details resulted in a great peace of mind, even in light of what it all meant. We were preparing for the end. We were preparing for me to be a widow.

PART TWO

The Middle Years: Living With Dementia

CHAPTER 6

Adjusting to a New Life

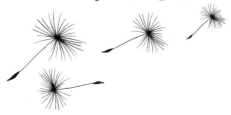

ONCE THE DIAGNOSIS had settled into the depths of our hearts and spirits, the day-to-day living with dementia began. We fell into a rhythm of daily activities. I went to work and Dan stayed at home tinkering with who knows what.

For a while it was kind of a blessing. I went to work and didn't worry too much about him. He would clean up the yard and flower beds and kept our house picked up by emptying the dishwasher or running the sweeper. I would call at lunchtime and do a check-in, and he would generally be in a good mood and list all the things he was doing. We seemed to sit on that plateau for about another 18 months.

Then things started to slide a bit more downhill. I would come home to messes and his high anxiety. Some days, I would pull into the garage and he would be standing there waiting for me with big wild eyes, revealing that something happened. I began to worry more about what he was up to than the tasks in my management job. I found myself calling him several times a day, and I would internally freak out if he wouldn't answer. He hadn't been able to text in quite a while, but usually he would answer the phone. Now he couldn't find his phone.

I was fortunate to have a very dear friend, Carol, living right next door whom I would occasionally call and ask her to check on him. She would call me back and tell me that she could see him raking leaves, mowing or standing in the driveway staring. Oh, that staring, I knew it well. Too well.

> ... *The blank stare. That is one part of dementia that haunts me daily. When he looks at me, it's as if he's looking right through me. Whatever happened to those sparkling eyes with a hint of mischief that made my heart melt? Since he's no longer allowed to drive, I found him just sitting in his van today, staring. I wonder what's going through his mind. I wonder if anything is going on in there. That sickening and unsettling feeling is churning in my gut. He's slipping away from me, a bit more, every single day.*

Eventually I came to the realization that I couldn't continue in the job I loved. The thought hit me like a lightning bolt one sleepless night. I met with my current boss and told him that we needed to prepare for my replacement, as I didn't feel I was giving my all to the job, while worrying all day what he was up to. I worried about the water left running, the refrigerator or freezer door left open, finding the hidden keys to his van and taking off. But mostly I was worried that he would hurt himself. I never knew what I would face when I came home. Some days were ok, but others would find him in a panic over what he lost or accidentally broke. I imagined things like getting his hand or foot caught in the lawn mower. It was time for me to say goodbye to a job of 40 years that I loved. I loved him more.

Plans were made, meetings with Human Resources occurred, and a replacement was selected. But like all plans made when dealing with dementia, they had to be adjusted to deal with his decline. Originally, I was to stay on six more months to train and work side-by-side with my successor, but after a few months, it was clear that I was needed more at home, and my early retirement date was moved up. Yes, there was resentment. I had always wanted to go out on my terms. In a way I did, but five years earlier than I had wanted or hoped. The health-care system I worked for was very fair and good to me, offering a severance package, which helped immensely. For that, I will always be grateful.

It was quite an adjustment being a retired person, and my internal alarm still went off at 5:30 every morning. But he was a late sleeper, and I learned to use that time to ready myself for the day and have a couple of hours to sip my coffee and revel in the peace and quiet.

We settled into somewhat of a routine, but perpetually adjusted the sails when there was a new loss of abilities or mood shift. I learned to celebrate the status quo because I knew that, sooner or later, a new loss would surface.

> … *The road of dementia is like a rocky descent down a mountain. Sometimes it feels like days, months, and maybe a year or more goes by and you don't notice a change.*
>
> *Then, all of a sudden, you repel down in an unexpected decline. You were just getting used to the new norm.*

Then BAM! You've hit another loss and you have to reset your life-line.

There are those periods when you think you've been on even ground forever, but then you reflect back and realize the losses that crept in unnoticed.

It rips your heart out and makes you numb and lost in the reality of just how far he's fallen. So, I tell myself to hang on to those good days that feel like I'm navigating smoothly and rest in between the falls.

CHAPTER 7

Perpetual Loss and Grief

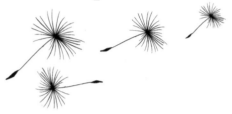

WHEN SOMEONE HAS DEMENTIA, there is so much uncertainty as to what your future will look like. But one certainty is clear. There will be continuous loss. Some will be great and dramatic. Some will be small and go unnoticed until you look at them in retrospect and collectively.

> … I've noticed that this staggering heat of late has really affected Dan. The hotter the day, the more tired and frustrated he seems to be. He tries to get his own shirt or socks on, but can't. This causes a big temper flare. I try to push fluids to keep him hydrated, but he often resists and says I'm trying to drown him.

It generally doesn't take long to figure out the loss of the day. Sometimes they hit you like a smack in the face, but often they're smaller things that signal, once again, the slow decline is real. We don't always connect the dots because they're little life skills that we take for granted.

... Today I realized that he couldn't figure out how to pull the tab to open a soda can. By the time I found him, he was trying to bang open the can with a pliers. One mess prevented.

... My heart hurts today when I realized that his FTD doesn't prevent him from realizing his deficits. As awful as it is for me as a caregiver, it has to be so very frightening for him, knowing that his mind is slowly melting away. His brain is becoming Swiss cheese. I hope that the next time I want to go postal on him, I'll remember that he hates this as much as I do.

Many caregivers compare their adult loved one with dementia to a toddler. They need help with dressing, showering, and eating. They are often selfish, and they want what they want when they want it. I disagree. Sure, toddlers can be all of those things, but so much more! You look forward to their milestones – walking, talking, going potty, and they reward you with a big hug and sloppy kisses, reminding you that you are the center of their world.

With dementia, there is continuous loss of independence and life skills, and often little to no empathy or expressions of love. Their memories gradually fade, as do their abilities to find words or grasp simple conversations. You lose them a thousand different ways on a thousand different days. You lose them long before they're gone. Looking back, I wish I had recorded conversations with Dan before he greatly declined. I would love to hear his voice today, although I do have one saved voicemail.

We all have those bless your heart moments. They usually come when they are trying so hard to be helpful. I distinctly recall a day when I wasn't feeling great and was trying to get our laundry done. Dan offered to put the clothes in the dryer for me. I gladly accepted his offer, but also reminded him to throw in a dryer sheet. An hour later, I went to retrieve the clothes to fold them, only to find no clothes in the dryer. But there was, however, a thoroughly dried dryer sheet that had been tossed around by itself for an hour. The clothes were still in the washer. Another bless your heart moment was when he told me he made coffee. I was so giddy that he had been able to do that as he proudly brought me a cup. It turned out, however, that it was quite gritty because he never put in a filter.

> *… The losses seem to be multiplying lately and I've noticed that he rarely offers to help anymore. I wish I had treasured and embraced those times that he helped instead of being annoyed by them. He has become more nonverbal and immobile. What I wouldn't give to go back and see that well-dried dryer sheet.*

The executive function losses can be the most annoying. To me, they seemed like such simple tasks and concepts. It's so hard to understand the effects of his brain's short circuiting.

> *… Irony. That's my word and thought for today. It's ironic that my husband who constantly harped at our kids and me about leaving lights on, now leaves every light on in the house every single day. I'm incessantly flipping off switches.*
>
> *It's ironic that the man who timed showers and made sure that the dishwasher and washing machine had*

full loads is now leaving the water running in every faucet in the house.

It's ironic that the guy who admonished us for hanging on an open refrigerator door looking for a snack is now the guy who gets a snack and walks away, leaving the door wide open.

The real irony of it all is that he is unfazed that we are single-handedly keeping the utility companies in business.

One glaring loss for those with dementia is the complete inability to recognize dates and times. Dan also had the concept that everything you talked about doing or upcoming events were happening right now.

… You'd think I'd learn not to talk about an appointment scheduled for tomorrow, next week or even next month, until it's almost time to get ready. As soon as I mention it, he's pacing around, getting anxious and wanting to leave right away. It doesn't help to remind him that it's not happening now, because in ten minutes, he'll be at it again.

It also doesn't matter if it's snowing on the first day of winter because he feels winter will be over tomorrow, and I need to get the lawn mower serviced and ready today. To everything there is a season, and that season will change again tomorrow.

Grief comes from all the things you've both lost – jobs, driving, freedom, conversation, friends, plans for the future. The list is endless. Some days the grief of the whole situation can be overwhelming. Some days it catches you off guard and you feel that lump in your throat and stab in your gut. Your chest tightens up and it feels like you can't take another step.

> ... *The grief of all the losses is hitting me hard today. But he's still here. Still painfully here. I miss having him drive me around like Miss Daisy. I miss him being able to help around the house. I miss his corny jokes that I've heard a hundred times. What I wouldn't give to hear them one more time. I hate him being in this condition, but he doesn't like it either. We are both frustrated, angry, sad, and scared.*
>
> *Dementia has got to be the most gut-wrenching disease to confront. It comes with a fatal diagnosis and you feel like you're in quicksand and slowly sinking into a dark abyss.*
>
> *As a caregiver, I feel like I'm being sucked through a mental and physical meat grinder. Every day seems to drain me more and more, while I watch him lose more and more abilities. I'm losing my partner more each day. I have no idea how long this will last, only that it will end.*
>
> *Some days it's so hard to get past this grief. But at the heart of it is a reminder that where there is great grief, there is great love.*

Life is random and unpredictable, and I don't like random and unpredictable. I like things to happen in a planned order, wrapped up in a bow. Being a dementia caregiver is super random and unpredictable. Seriously, my best laid plans often blew up without a moment's notice. I learned over time to stay on my toes and to pivot every time a new loss or challenge showed up. Eventually, I did become an expert at expecting the unexpected and being able to go with the flow.

> … I've always been a list maker. You know, so I can check things off. Dementia laughs at my lists, spits on them and crumples them up into a ball, and throws them at me. This whole journey is not in my nature, but maybe is God's way of teaching me patience and not to fight the tide of constant change and loss.

CHAPTER 8

Finding Humor

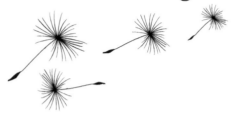

BELIEVE IT OR NOT, it's possible and crucial to find laughter in living with dementia. Learning to laugh in the unexpected moments is essential to surviving. Look for those random opportunities to find humor in moments you'd rather cry.

In one of the earlier years of his illness, we decided to take a weekend trip to southwest Pennsylvania. We loved searching the back roads for historic covered bridges, and this area had many of them. The winding, desolate roads proved to be more difficult than expected, and we eventually discovered that we were lost. I started to get nervous giggles as I drove the narrow, stony paths, while he turned the map upside down and sideways. When I saw a car with West Virginia plates in front of an isolated house, I knew we were way off course. I drove a little farther and stopped the car. We both got out, walked around and stared down a really steep ravine.

Dan said, "This is how you're going to do it, isn't it?"

I replied, "Do what?"

He said, "Get rid of me. I knew you've been watching all of those crime shows for a reason. They'll never find my body down there."

We both had a good laugh and eventually found our way back to civilization because I took over the map.

> *... Sometimes I feel like I should rename us Pete and Repeat. I tire of having the same questions asked again and again, or the same stories told over and over. It can be exasperating.*
>
> *But I often feel like Repeat as I do a certain task again and again. Sometimes I wonder if I'M the one losing it. I take outgoing mail to the mailbox, only to find it back on the kitchen table. So, I return it to the mailbox, and a few minutes later, he brings it back again. Ok. Now it's a game. I'll need to distract him and time it so that I take it out just before the mailman comes. I'm feeling up to the challenge.*

I'm an avid essential oil user and frequently try different blends in my diffuser to aid in lowering his anxiety – or mine! I came across a funny post on Facebook that made me giggle. It said: Essential oil friends – Which oil calms household family members down? Chloroform? It's Chloroform, isn't it?

> *... Even though that still makes me giggle, we all can seriously relate. It seems that we often chase the magic combination of meds to help reduce his anxiety and find peace and balance. Some days we are successful, some days – not so much. On those days we may be rifling through our essential oils wishing we had that potion that would just freaking calm him down.*

Living with someone who has aphasia with their dementia brings another level of humor. You feel helpless when they're word-searching and their anxiety level is rising. It reminds me of that game show *Password*. Your loved one gives you one-word subtle clues here and there, and you hang on until it hits you like a eureka moment. Then you blurt out the answer and their eyes light up like you just won the grand prize. But often you blurt out the wrong answer, and they stomp their feet and pound their fists. That's the parting gift you get for giving a completely bogus answer. But seriously, the longer you play the game, the better you get at gleaning together their fractured thoughts.

Some days you really need to dig for that humor to get you through. For me, it would be the days that he had to have fasting lab work and x-rays (for his autoimmune disease). Trying to keep someone with dementia from eating during those fasting hours is a whole new level of strategic planning. He can't figure out how to open the refrigerator door – except when he can't have anything to eat. So, for 12 hours and straight through the night, his mantra was, "Why can't I eat? I want to eat. I want a cookie. You're mean!

"Yes, I am mean."

I wanted to give a cookie to the poor phlebotomist. She would straighten his arm and he would bend it. I helped hold it straight. Then she put on the bandage and he immediately ripped it off and blood spurted everywhere. She put on another bandage and he ripped it off and stuck it on her lab coat pocket. So, a third one went on and I held it in place with the promise of a cookie coming soon. Getting the chest x-ray done was another whole battle. But we finished, and even though he had very little short-term memory, he remembered to keep asking for that damn promised cookie.

... Come one, come all, to the greatest crap show on earth! I often feel like I'm the ringmaster in some bizarre circus. But the budget is really low, so you not only have to be the ringmaster, but the tightrope walker, the animal trainer, the really bad fortune teller, the clown, and the dart thrower. It's really a two-person show with no audience.

Production begins every morning and continues throughout the day with unexpected surprises and clean-up calls.

Then, as with all great shows, there must be a grand finale. This involves chaos and sundowning, which will keep you on your toes until the final curtain closes. No, we don't want an encore, just a quiet circus tent through the night.

Dementia caregivers live a life that even fiction novelists would scoff at. We ponder bewildering questions that others never need to entertain.

If you're out and about with your loved one of the opposite sex and they need to use the bathroom, do you take them into the women's or men's, if there is no family restroom available? Do you wait for an 'all clear' or announce that you're entering with the opposite sex? If you're inside the stall with them, can you imagine what someone just entering will hear and think? ("Let me get your zipper. Point it to the hole. No, we're not playing games now.")

... If you don't learn to see the humor in life with dementia, you'll drive yourself insane. This is the crazy life we

live. We are warriors. We are adapters. We are the problem solvers. We should run for office.

... There are so many valuable life lessons you learn while caring for someone with dementia. Did you know:

If you put a can of soda in the freezer, it will explode?

If you put the ice cube bucket in the fridge, the ice will melt?

If you put a metal cup in the microwave, it will start a fire?

If you use Gorilla Glue to secure the top of a flashlight, you can't get it open to change the batteries?

If you don't plug in a fan, it won't work, no matter how much you scream profanities at it?

If you soak the tube of toothpaste in a sink full of hot water, the toothpaste will run out of it like water when you take off the lid?

If you don't put the carafe under the coffeemaker, you will have coffee everywhere except in the carafe?

For these and other scientific facts, stay tuned, or live with someone who has dementia.

CHAPTER 9
Strength, Courage and Resilience

I F YOU'RE CARING FOR SOMEONE WITH DEMENTIA, you will be told repeatedly, "You're so strong!" I'm sure it's meant as a compliment and to make you feel like a super hero, but this is what I heard: "Thank God it's you and not me."

Okay, so maybe we've conditioned ourselves to bear more stress than the average Joe, but my shoulders got pretty darn tired of having to do so. Many of us caregivers may appear strong when putting on our warrior faces, but too often we cry into pillows or in the shower when we can feel our weaknesses. We may be strong, but we're really just dealing with the crappy hands we've been dealt with as much grace and dignity as possible.

> *… If what doesn't kill you makes you stronger, I should be able to bench press a bulldozer by now. Seriously, people constantly tell me that I'm so strong. I get tired of being strong. I want to have at least one week of being weak.*
>
> *But in reality, I know that I'm stronger than I thought I ever could be. Yes, the tears sometimes flow freely, but that's because the pain is real. I try to keep going*

in the midst of the pain and frustration. I clean up one more mess. I watch our friends going about normal daily life activities. I substitute our social calendars for doctors' appointments, showering, dressing and feeding. I learn how to do it all, including which adult diapers provide the best results. I feel broken and can only hope that I will blossom into a strong and resilient warrior.

Journalist Charles M. Blow said, "One doesn't have to operate with great malice to do great harm. The absence of empathy and understanding are sufficient." Never have there been wiser words. As a caregiver, you operate with great empathy. You make endless changes and sacrifices, and alter steps and care plans to make things go as smoothly as possible. Your heart sinks with every new loss and frustration. You, all too well, understand how difficult tasks become for them and the mental exhaustion they go through.

But, when the shoe is on the other foot and you are ill, hurting, frustrated or grieving, it's exceptionally hard to not receive any empathy or understanding.

… As Dan loses his capacity for empathy, I seem to parallel it with my own degree of numbness. It has become my shield against the hurt, pain, anger and grief. It becomes my safe space.

But as time marches on and on, year after year, that numbing coping skill becomes the norm in my personality. I don't want it to. I don't want to end my time on earth being cynical, unfeeling or bitter. Yes, that numb feeling is safer, less traumatizing, but I want to be able to love and have that love reciprocated. When this terrible chapter passes, I want to feel less traumatized, more healed, and ready to feel good and bad emotions. Maybe I need to start today by not hiding all of my emotions. Maybe I need to occasionally acknowledge that I'm hurting. Maybe I need to show a crack in my shell.

That's why it's so important to have the right support person in your life. Someone who will be your cheerleader. Someone who will let you vent and not judge. Someone who can help you be strong... one more day. Because some days the anger is so powerful that it's hard to smile and accept well-meaning bits of advice from friends and family who have no idea what it's like to deal with this 24/7.

... I don't want to hear how strong I am. I don't want to be reminded that God never gives us more than we can handle. You'll get your reward in heaven. You're never given more than you can carry. Take one day at a time. Put one foot in front of the other. I'd like to tell them where to put that foot. Seriously, I know they mean well, and it's their way of trying to be helpful, but they're not.

When you feel so desolate, alone and angry, their clichés are not helpful. I know that this too shall pass. But right now, that is one more freaking quote I don't want to hear.

Caregivers give all they can to their loved ones. However, there are times when we so badly want someone to take care of us.

Then, that self-realization makes us feel guilty, selfish, and weak all at once. Most of us were raised to not depend on others to make us happy and to handle all the sh** that life shovels on top of us.

> … *I am often called a strong woman. I know that's meant to be a compliment, but more often than not, it's like fingernails on a chalkboard. I no longer want to be strong. I'm tired of being strong. Many days, I crave to be the one being taken care of instead of always being the caretaker. Where do I sign up for the weak, or at least the non-super hero club? It would be a welcome change to have someone wait on me, cook for me, clean up my messes, pay the bills, organize appointments, medications, and just generally do everything.*
>
> *The lack of empathy from my partner in life is so disheartening and I often don't feel very strong. I cry in silence and feel very weak. But then I look in his eyes and know that I am his one constant source of comfort and strength.*

A year before Dan passed, my long-term chronic back pain came to a head. I had put off surgery for many years because I was taking care of him. But it got to the point that I would sit or lie down and cry because the pain was so bad. I was so miserable that I was short-fusing every time he made a mess or annoyed me. So, plans were made to have my surgery and the girls and I decided to place him in memory care for two weeks, starting with the day before my procedure. After dropping him off and getting him settled, I bawled all the way home. I kept picturing his eyes pleading to take him with me.

Kelly accompanied me the day of my surgery and my sister, Pat, brought me home three days later. Becky stayed with me the first night and then others checked on me over the next few days.

It was a painful surgery and a very difficult recovery, but I was able to have two weeks of being tended to instead of being the caregiver. The care center would put Dan on the phone so he could hear my voice, and then he would cry and beg to come home. Each day I would tell him how many more days, and he would always tell me that was too many. Once he did come home, I had to go back as the caregiver as well as endure months of spinal surgery recovery. Talk about being strong!

Many times, I would vent to my family member or friends how bad his condition was, often through drenching tears and total despair. They would tell me it was time to place him in memory care. But mentally, I wasn't there yet. Every day wasn't bad. But there were some pretty awful moments. What I wanted from them was an opportunity to vent and maybe see that I was reaching out for some much-needed relief now and then.

Please know that we are worthy of being taken care of, and the continual denial of admitting this will result in being overtaken by loneliness and despair. So, this is my plea, from one caregiver to another. Reach out for help from your family, friends, church or a counselor. You may need to be specific. You deserve to be cared for and there are many people who want to be of service, but are afraid to intrude. Welcome the intrusion. Make that request.

CHAPTER **10**

The Anchors

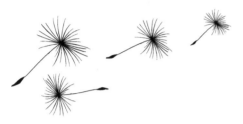

WHEN NAVIGATING THROUGH A STORM LIKE DEMENTIA, you will find along the way those true gems who are your anchors. Never underestimate their value. They are the people who help you get through the toughest of days and give you the strength to face another one. Our family worked together against the FTD war. We were all in the battle but Dan was the one who took the bullet. Nonetheless, it took our little village to endure the fight.

We had the unfortunate presence of the Covid-19 pandemic occurring at the same time as one of the last years of his illness. As if dementia isn't isolating enough, throw the quarantining of a pandemic in the mix and you have the perfect storm for epic loneliness. You would think that we would have already been professional isolators, just with the dementia alone. But add a pandemic to a situation with a long-term terminal illness, and stir-crazy doesn't begin to describe it.

We were fortunate to stay relatively healthy throughout the pandemic and were blessed with so many angels who reached out the best they could. It was not unusual to find treats on our front porch, special gifts delivered to lift our spirits, and even full meals from time to time. When we canceled our annual family Thanksgiving, a neighbor showed up with two complete turkey dinners with all the trimmings. After a big snow, our driveway would be plowed without having to ask. Our daughters Face-Timed us through the worst of it and kept us supplied in groceries. People offered to come and visit, but Dan was super paranoid about either of us getting sick. Just the thought of visitors coming in sent him into a high anxiety panic. So those first few months, we were pretty much isolated, but as the weather grew warmer, I allowed people to come in and visit, albeit at a distance.

My next-door neighbor, Carol, was one of my main anchors. When the toughest of days got the best of me, I would walk next door, stand in the middle of her living room and vent, cry and even scream the F-bomb. She would tell me to yell it at the top of my lungs. I'd get all cried out, back under control, and return home with a smile.

My mom, who is currently 96, was my stronghold. She lived only a mile away and I felt safe to cry on her shoulder and glean all the wisdom from someone who had been widowed at the age of 60 when my dad died of cancer. She understood. She worried about me. It was nice to have someone worry about me.

I had several friends who checked on me regularly, dropped off care packages, but mostly just let me know that they cared and were there if needed. Some helped me figure out how to fix things around the house or gave advice and physical help whenever needed. Several of these friends did so without being asked.

One special gem, Joyce, came into our lives when we needed her the most. After having my much-needed back surgery and Dan coming home, Joyce blessed us with a couple of hours each day, two or three times a week to help him dress, shower, keep him company, do some laundry and make his breakfast. She regularly helped him organize his workshop, which meant watching him move things to new locations again and again and then often back to the original place. When I told her that I wished I had her patience, she said, "Mary, I get to go home. You don't."

After I was getting around better, Joyce stayed on with us one day a week for another 10 months until Dan went into permanent memory care. This allowed me to get groceries, have lunch out, visit my mom or just take a walk in a park. She was truly a godsend. Dan grew very attached to her and they became best buddies, even though he could never remember her name. He always called her Janice. I even wrote JOYCE in big letters on the grease board on the front of our fridge to remind him.

He looked forward to their Wednesday afternoons together. When he asked me when she was coming next, I would wink at him and ask, "Who are you talking about?" He would walk to the fridge, look at her name and point to it. But in the next instance he would call her Janice again, smile, and know that wasn't right. It became comical. Everyone needs a Joyce. Or a Janice. Her peaceful manner and faith-filled heart helped keep my sails upright.

> … Dear God, before I lay my head down to rest tonight, I just want to say "Thank You." Thank you for sending the important anchors in our lives and helping us hold on in this ravaging storm. Sometimes my sails feel battered and torn, but you send us just what we need before our ship sinks. Tonight, I ask that you bless them, as you know who they are and the blessings they continue to give us.

Tomorrow may be another challenging day, but I'll close my eyes tonight and smile at all the God-wink moments you have sent to provide us with ports of respite.

Frustration, anger and resentment can become the norm for caregivers, especially when there is little to no relief. It builds layer after layer until it becomes unbearable. That's when we erupt and the process repeats. But, if the flare-ups become too frequent, they can be detrimental to you and your loved one. The constant anger and resentment can cause irreparable damage to our own health, as well as aggravate our loved one's anxiety and confusion.

Before the situation becomes like Old Faithful, seek counseling. I did. I found myself becoming angrier and more resentful. My patience with Dan was wearing thin, and I wasn't always very kind or understanding. Seeking help is not a sign of weakness but rather one of strength and courage. There is something so liberating and therapeutic about being able to vent what pushes your buttons and why you feel bitterness and rage. Love yourself enough to find someone who will listen and give you the tools to better cope with this heavy burden.

CHAPTER 11

Loss of Relationships

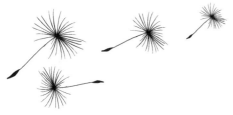

ONE OF THE MORE DIFFICULT ASPECTS OF DEMENTIA is the loss of friends, especially those people who have been around for years. Even after his death, it's still hard for me to come to terms with the feeling that Dan was abandoned by his closest friends. At the onset of his disease, I'm sure they thought he was just being quirky, laughed it off and kept coming around. But as the disease progressed, their visits became scarcer and then disappeared completely.

I know that many people don't know what to say, how to act, or what to do when someone's mind starts to go. If they only knew that we don't really care what they say or how they act. Do something. Do anything. Just do. When your loved one can no longer hold a conversation, their friends need to fill in the memory gaps and just be present.

It's extremely difficult to watch life go on while you are caring for your loved one. While scrolling through Facebook, I would see photos and stories of friends and families going on vacations, to ballgames, shows, or just out having fun. I was so envious of the normalcy of their lives. Yes, I know that most people only post their "good" lives and not their trials. But what I saw over and over was joy, adventure and freedom. I felt stuck, but I really didn't want to go do those things, at least not with my husband, or even without him, for that matter. Oh, we tried, but restaurant and ballgame experiences were mostly filled with high anxiety and difficulty with his mobility. It was not worth the effort. They were also filled with the looks of pity from people around us.

In the autumn of the year before he died, our grandson was playing for the championship midget football program. The Super Bowl of Midget Football! I wanted to go watch him in the worst way, and Dan said he wanted to go, too. So, I dressed us both in warm clothes and made the hour trip to the game. Parking was a nightmare. No handicapped spaces were to be found. I ended up dropping him off near the entrance gate and instructed him to stay right there until I returned. When I finally got up to the gate, I couldn't find him. Luckily, someone we knew guided me to where he had wandered. Going up the bleacher steps was difficult but we made it. He had no idea what was going on during the whole game but didn't complain. He just sat there totally oblivious that we had won the game.

When it was over, we waited a while, allowing people to empty out of the stands because we knew it was going to be difficult getting him down. As I finally talked him into trying, he couldn't figure out how to go down the aisle steps. He was starting to panic and a couple of people whom we knew well, ignored us. Some kind strangers stepped in and tried to help. He got angrier and angrier wanting to do it himself. As people started coming into the stands for the next game, I began to panic, too, wondering how we would ever get him down. Somehow, by a sheer miracle, we were finally able to coax him down. But by then, he was so frustrated, embarrassed and angry. I was afraid to leave him alone to get the car, so I had no choice but to make him walk quite a distance with me. Then he couldn't figure out how to get into the car. When he was eventually in, I buckled him up and vowed I would never put either of us in that situation again. We became even more isolated in our safe place at home.

The abandonment by long-term friends hurts the caregiver as much as the one with dementia – probably more. Dan did have a few old friends from high school whom he hadn't seen in years. They showed up for visits, which meant the world to both of us. He never lost his long-term memory and loved listening to old stories of their mischievous childhoods. Even on one occasion, a couple of his old co-workers took him out to lunch. But his present-day friends were gone. What he wouldn't have given to have them come and talk about their fish stories and that big one that got away.

My sweet Dan was the one who helped all the new fishermen. He gave them lessons, free tackle, welcomed them as his partner on his boat in tournaments, and spent endless time with them. He was the mentor, always wanting to help and teach. When he became the one in need, no one showed up.

> *… I try very hard not to hold a grudge against Dan's friends who have abandoned him. I know that they probably feel uncomfortable and don't know what to say or do. But my dear hubby is still here. The man I love and the friend they liked to swap amusing stories with is still in there. My heart breaks for him in his loneliness.*

My hope is that if I learn one thing from this night-mare, it's that I will become a better friend, a better listener, a better do-er.

I have asked God to forgive me for the anger I feel about this issue. I'm still a work in progress on that one.

CHAPTER 12

The Well-Intended Ones

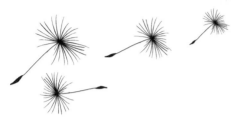

THROUGHOUT THOSE LONG 10 YEARS, there were the anchors, the disappointers, and the well-intended ones who graced us with loads of unsolicited advice. Often, they were like fingernails on a chalkboard, but I had mastered the grateful smile.

My favorite ones were those early on, when someone would visit and when I walked them out to their car, would say, "Well, he seems fine to me. Maybe he was just having a few bad days." They had their whole one-hour experience with him, so they should know! Try spending 24/7 with him a few days and then tell me just how fine he is.

The other one I heard so frequently was, "I know just how you feel. My grandma had Alzheimer's, too." I'm sure they understood completely. Grandma was 87 and Dan was 60. Oh, by the way, he doesn't have Alzheimer's. He has FTD. Yes, they're both a type of dementia but two different animals.

… I know that people don't mean to be insensitive, but some of their comments make me want to hurl. Here are some of the better ones I heard:

- *You are so strong. You can handle this.*
- *Oh, I make mistakes and forget things, too.*
- *This too shall pass. (Seriously, what the hell?!)*
- *Everything happens for a reason.*
- *Isn't he better yet? (One of the best!)*
- *He seems all right to me.*
- *I know just how you feel.*
- *God Bless You. You're in our prayers. (Again, well-intended and I don't know why this one bothers me.)*
- *Was he a drinker? I've heard that causes it.*
- *Don't let it get you down.*
- *They may find a cure any day.*
- *So, you retired early. Lucky you! You're living the dream! (Yes, a nightmare!)*
- *God never gives you more than you can handle.*
- *Make sure you're taking care of yourself.*
- *Dementia is just another way of thinking.*
- *Isn't he sweet? Just like a three-year-old.*
- *He's trying so hard. Be nice to him.*
- *He's just depressed. Have you tried medications?*
- *Are you sure it's not just a mean streak or a phase he's going through?*
- *Maybe you should try Ginkgo.*

To try and be fair, it's not really what we don't like to hear that should be emphasized but what we would like. Here are some ideas:

- You have your hands full. I can't imagine, but I'm just a phone call away if you need to vent.
- I will be here on this date and time to sit with your loved one for a couple of hours so that you can get away.
- We will be bringing supper tomorrow and visiting.
- I plan to mow your yard this week and clean your gutters.
- Let me take him for a drive and some ice cream.
- I'd like to pick up some groceries for you.
- We will be there to visit with both of you.

So, the big lesson here is: Actions speak louder than words.

We all get loads of advice as to what would help us or our loved one. Bless their hearts. They mean well. Well, most of them do. But in the end, it's our job to make decisions in their best interests. It takes a while to get to the point that you can say, "It's my decision. I have to live with this every day and I know best." Maybe you truly don't know best, but you know in your heart what is best for you and your loved one in that moment.

It's ok for others to be supportive and have an opinion, but it is NOT ok for them to approve or disapprove of your decisions. You are the one who is dealing with it ALL! Set the tone early in the disease. Tell them that they can best help you by listening, offering advice when asked, and supporting your decisions after they have been made. Because once they leave, you are the one who must deal with the cold and hard reality.

CHAPTER 13

Those Trying Tiring Days

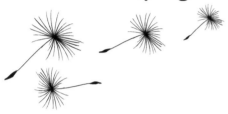

SOME DAYS ARE JUST HARDER THAN OTHERS. These are the days when he is more confused, more fatigued, paranoid and short-fused. These are the days when even those who are giving me a couple of hours away, cannot wait to exit our home. These are the days that he himself becomes completely frustrated and broken.

Frustration is a word that became a common staple in my vocabulary. I got frustrated when I explained something over and over without any positive result or understanding. I got frustrated when I would tell him something and he repeated it to someone else in a completely false narrative. I got frustrated when I had to clean up the tenth spill of the day or only got to play 'the find part' of hide-and-seek. I got frustrated when he would undo all the work put into getting him dressed or cleaned.

But as frustrated as I became in all the things he couldn't do, I couldn't imagine how totally exasperated he must have gotten at no longer being able to do them. He was always the go-to guy, Mr. Fixit. I have no shame in saying that he babied me, worried about me, and always tried to take care of everything he could around the house. With dementia, he would often shed a tear, saying that he didn't feel like a man anymore.

> *... I feel so bad for him, as everything seems to be a battle – getting dressed, shaving, showering, getting a drink. I woke up to no hot water because he had unplugged the water heater for some unknown reason. He spilled over half a gallon of iced tea on the kitchen floor this morning. I walked into the kitchen an hour after cleaning up that mess to find half a bag of potato chips all over the floor. He just looked at me and said that he had a problem with the bag. After searching for my hair conditioner that is always in the shower, I found it on a bookshelf in the hallway. He told me he put it there because it was lotion. Makes no sense and he looks at me with that helpless plea. Later today, I found clumps of poop in the bathroom sink. He had no idea how they got there.*
>
> *I'm exhausted, angry and so very frustrated. And yet, I know that things will continue to only get worse. I can't begin to imagine. All day, he looked tired and confused and struggled mightily with word searching. We've both had enough of this nightmare for one day.*
>
> *There was a book that was quite popular in 1967 titled: I'm OK – You're OK by Thomas Anthony Harris. I couldn't tell you what it was about, but for some reason, that title has stuck in my brain.*
>
> *Well, let me tell you something. If you've cared for a loved one with dementia 24/7 for years, you've experienced those really bad days, and you live by this motto: He/*

She Isn't OK – and I'm Not OK. Some days, I'm almost appalled at how 'not ok' I am.

But do you know what? I'm telling you right now that it's perfectly ok to not be ok, because this whole situation is not ok, and we do the best we can. If today we didn't do ok, God will give us a whole new day tomorrow for a fresh start. The sun will come up again, and we'll have another chance to be ok ... or not.

I once saw a post on Facebook that really struck me hard and stayed with me on those trying days. It said: Here's to another day of outward smiles and inward screams.

... God love him when he's being all sweet and helpful. But be afraid. Be very afraid. After I spent a day making jam and was left with all the kitchen mess that goes with it, I cleaned and cleaned but the floor still felt sticky. My sweet hubby announced that he would take care of it for me and I should go stretch out in my recliner. I didn't bat an eye because I was bone tired.

When I later returned to the kitchen, I found a mess that could only be described as a flour bomb that had exploded. Oh, but no, he had sprinkled body powder over everything because that always helps him when he feels sticky.

Like I said, be afraid.

Many of us were raised to suffer in silence and put on a happy face. Don't show your inner turmoil. Pull up your big girl pants and just deal with it. God forbid that anyone sees your human side. I may have been brought up that way, but my face shows every emotion. I either look like the happy Labrador Retriever with his tail wagging and tongue hanging out or like the sad St. Bernard who lost his best friend. That's how I survived the chaos. I learned over the years to try and control my frustration and sadness when I was around Dan, but being human, I failed time and again. But I also learned to forgive myself. I have lost my temper with him, and I've yelled, cussed and had tantrums. But I reminded myself that I was dealing with an impossible situation. After the guilt set in and I calmed down, I always asked for his forgiveness. When we're tired and scared, anger and resentment rear their ugly heads.

I was his wife. I vowed in sickness and in health, till death do us part. It's so hard in those very trying days to remember that I'm still his wife, not just his caretaker.

> ... I'm still his wife. I often need to remind myself. Some days, it's just not as clear. So, I'll repeat the mantra again and again, so that I don't forget.
>
> As I tell him that he's beginning to smell ripe and it's time to shower, I'm still his wife. As I clip his nails and shave his face, I'm still his wife. When I put his shoes on the right feet and shirt right side out, I'm still his wife. When he's sitting on his bed pouting because he didn't get his way, I'm still his wife. When I fix the TV channel for the umpteenth time, I'm still his wife. When I celebrate his birthday but mine goes unnoticed and unremembered again, I'm still his wife.
>
> When I tuck him in at night and he smiles and says, "Thank you," I'm still his wife.

CHAPTER **14**

Challenging Holidays

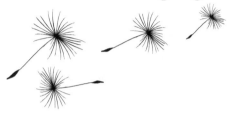

HOLIDAYS, BIRTHDAYS AND ANNIVERSARIES can be quite challenging, especially the further your loved one's dementia progresses. First of all, when the day arrives, you never know if it's going to be a good day, bad day, high anxiety day or sleepy day. On top of that, their mood can change in a heartbeat.

When Dan's birthday rolled around, I always decided to celebrate with as much normalcy as possible. No big party, probably a cake, and I encouraged cards and phone calls. I tried to discourage crowds because they tended to make him more anxious and confused. One of his last years, I shared a post on Facebook encouraging people to send him a humorous card because he still loved a good joke and a laugh.

> … *After securing all the birthday cards that came in the mail, I surprised him today with a big pile of cards from friends and family. He sat there and fumbled with them, lifting them up and shuffling them around – over and over. I finally figured out that he had no clue how to open them. I wanted to cry. I sat with him then and opened*

one at a time and read each out loud because he could no longer read. He would smile here and there, but mostly had that blank stare. I wanted to go outside and scream. Another loss.

As dementia marched on, year after year, our anniversary became less of a blip on the radar. Before FTD, he NEVER forgot our anniversary. We weren't into gifts, but we would get silly cards for each other. Well, actually, he usually got me two cards – one sappy and one silly. When he got to the point that I knew he had no concept of dates, I would tell him it was our anniversary. So that he wouldn't feel bad, I'd say that I hadn't had time to get him a card, so we'd just have a nice dinner that evening. He would smile and be satisfied.

… Today was our 43rd anniversary. Since cards are way over his capability now, I didn't buy one, either, but suggested we order curbside from Applebee's. He liked that idea and I pulled up their menu online. I gave him several suggestions, but ended up just picking something out for both of us. As I started to enter the order, he says, "I just want an Arby's sandwich." Ok. Plan B. We drove to Arby's and ordered sandwiches and fries at the drive-thru. He no longer does well inside restaurants. If I've learned anything from FTD, it's how to go with the flow and flip on a dime.

The big three holidays – Thanksgiving, Christmas and Easter – were always held at our home and the kids and grandkids came with all the fanfare and energy that little ones bring. Somewhere along the way, probably in the last four or five years, it was just too much for him. We have a small ranch home and there's nowhere to escape when it all gets too overwhelming. So, the girls started alternating hosting those holiday gatherings. They had larger homes and if it all got to be too much for Dan, I could simply take him home.

When it came to my birthday, the goal was to keep it under wraps. If he found out and had nothing to give me, he would cry and pout. So, cards were hidden, and I instructed other family and friends not to acknowledge my day in front of him.

> … *My plan to keep my birthday a secret went without a hitch today until his brother came over for a visit. As soon as he sat down, he said, "Happy Birthday, Mary!" Dan immediately looked over at me and started tearing up. I downplayed it with my best poker face saying, "I didn't want to have one this year. I'm getting too old!" By the time his brother left, he forgot all about it. But as I finished tucking him in tonight and looked in the mirror at my tired face, I couldn't hold back the tears. Another whisper that he's leaving me.*

I will always have a favorite holiday story. About two years before he died, I took him to our local big box store to get groceries. As we walked in, there were hundreds of beautiful floral bouquets and boxes of candy. He asked what the occasion was, and I said, "Valentine's Day."

He asked if he could get flowers for me, and I replied that I appreciated the thought but it wasn't necessary. He stood and pouted and refused to move. So, I told him to pick out some flowers. He managed to pick out the biggest and prettiest bunch in the display. He walked around the store proudly holding them and told people that he was buying them for his Valentine.

About 10 minutes before we were done shopping, he literally threw the bouquet into my cart and said he would pay for them himself. I knew he had no money, so I said that I would give him some when we got to the register. By the time I got there, he was wandering off to look at something else and forgot all about them. So, I paid for the flowers and the groceries, wrangled him back, and we walked to the car. There was never another mention of the flowers, even after I put them in a vase and proudly displayed them on the table. Sometimes, you really do have to create your own special gifts.

> ... *Groundhog's Day should be declared a national holiday for dementia caregivers. We relive the same day over and over in a nightmarish loop. Unlike the movie, however, we don't have some sort of epiphany and everything resets with everyone living happily ever after.*
>
> *The monotony of our perpetual groundhog days is a double-edged sword. You get sick and tired of living the same ambiguous routine day after day, but you know that any change that occurs will be another decline with new and harder challenges. So, should I embrace these monotonous days and risk losing my own soul to any hope for the future? I think I'd rather have the cloudy day so that rodent won't see his shadow and hibernate any longer than necessary.*

CHAPTER 15

Creating Good Days

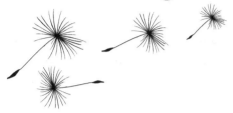

THERE ARE GOOD DAYS. Really there are. When you've been in this role for a long time, you learn to lower your expectations of what a good day looks like. It can mean no spills, nothing gets broken, no verbal altercations, or no hide-and-seek adventures. It can mean a little clarity, a conversation that makes sense, or no battles with dressing, showering or eating. A great day can mean an unexpected visit from an old friend.

I had many of those quality days, ones that came naturally. But sometimes I learned that I needed to create them. These involved quiet car rides, slow walks in a park, and hot fudge sundaes. Dan loved just riding around looking at the countryside. He would relax, smile and point things out along the way. I learned to bring a plastic bowl for his fast food or ice cream treat, or I'd be picking up French fries all over my car for months.

One cold December morning, we were both going a bit stir crazy, and I asked if he was up for doing something fun. His eyes lit up and he went for his coat. I packed a small cooler full of snacks, drinks and a fresh supply of wet wipes – necessary for any travel, not just for him because I'm messy, too. I had heard of a little candy store in New Weston, Ohio, called Birt's Store, about a 90-minute drive from home. It's literally the tiniest of dots on the map and the store IS the town. They have other bulk foods, but sugared treats is their main thing. It was small, crowded, and quite overwhelming for him, especially since we were still dealing with the Covid virus. I quickly chose some treats and got us out of there. He couldn't wait to dig into the candy. Our saying was always: If it has sugar, then he loves it. From there, we took a scenic drive around Grand Lake St. Mary's, amazed at the frozen water and waves of ice. We stopped at a park and ate the picnic lunch I had packed. We arrived home, both feeling a little refreshed and recharged. Well, maybe that was the sugar.

Another day trip took us to Independence Dam Park near Defiance, Ohio. We drove along the Maumee River from the dam to Grand Rapids, Ohio, enjoying the fall foliage, and then walked along the parks and looked in the shop windows. We took silly pictures to commemorate our special day. I found that he was much happier not having to deal with the formalities and the people in restaurants. Simply put, he enjoyed our being together. So did I.

I also found that I could turn a boring or bad day into a better one through music. It has always been an important part of our lives. Whenever we were in the car, we had music playing and we'd both sing along, especially to '50s and '60s tunes. Music improved our moods, and I knew that if I played our favorite songs, his anxiety would decrease and he would gradually relax. On good occasions, I could even get him to try to dance. It certainly didn't resemble our old steps, but we both embraced the closeness and a small sense of normalcy.

... Like music, life ebbs and flows. We have good days and bad. Some start like a slow dance, and others move on like Saturday Night Fever. Life as a caregiver only proves that the music will most certainly change. We can't choose the music that life plays for us, but we can choose how we dance to it.

Even though it's harder to find joy in some days more than others, I always tried to end each one reminiscing on something positive that happened. Sometimes I had to dig deep, really deep, but there was always something, and I praised God for that moment. Sometimes, I would take a deep breath and simply recognize that I was still breathing. He was still with me.

Life may be complicated, sad, and downright depressing at times, but I knew I couldn't park my carcass and live in that state forever. So yes, I wallowed in days of self-pity, anger and depression, but I also made positive choices to create joy for both of us.

... Today will be the best day Dan will probably ever have. Each passing day will bring more loss, so I chose to celebrate today. I chose to make memories, not for him, but for me. He won't remember beyond the smiles he gave me today when we walked around the park and ate ice cream. But I will. I made memories that I will carry through my grief when this journey is over.

CHAPTER 16

Dealing with Anger

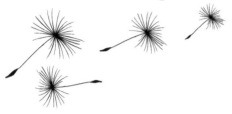

ONE OF THE HARDEST THINGS for me to deal with was his bouts of anger. Fortunately, this didn't happen often but when it did, it was scary and unsettling. It always came out of frustration. The kinds of matches that lit the fuse were when he tried repeatedly to put on his socks, or get a T-shirt on the right way, or his underwear pulled down before the pee came out.

Most of the time, I could talk him down. I usually made a joke about whatever the thing was and downplay it, which would calm him for that moment. But not always. There were a handful of times that I did fear for my safety. These were late in his disease and I don't think he even realized what he was doing most of the time. I remember one specific moment when I was trying to help him with his lunch and he kept making one mess after another. I was getting as upset as he was, but all of a sudden, he gritted his teeth, pulled back his arm and made a fist like he was going to punch me. I looked at him and simply said, "Go ahead. It will only take once and you won't get a second chance." He immediately stopped, put his arm down, and sulked in anger for over an hour.

There were a lot of screaming incidents. He would yell and even cuss at me when he thought I wasn't helping him enough, or I was helping him too much, or I wasn't letting him be a man. That last one was a big issue. Sometimes I could ease his anger but other times I locked myself in my room and bawled my eyes out. I know that really didn't help either of us but it's how I dealt with it at the time.

There was one specific time that his anger was so bad that I called his brother for help. He came and took him out to his workshop where Dan showered him with his wrath, as well. But then, all of a sudden, he just stopped. Apparently, the neurons were firing appropriately because he came into the house, with tears in his eyes, stood in front of me and said, "Honey, I'm so sorry." Broke my heart.

But what about the anger that we as caregivers experience? Some days I just felt in limbo, somewhere between losing my mind and losing my soul. There were so many times that I wanted, no NEEDED, to have a conversation with my husband, but he was no longer there mentally. So, I motored through the day in silence.

> *... The silence becomes deafening and I long so earnestly for any normal sense of adult conversation. But normal adults don't understand the depth of my despair and what it's doing to my general outlook on life. So, I remain silent.*

It's so important to give yourself permission to "feel the feels," and express what you need to say. If necessary, create a safe space where you can be honest with your emotions - journal, vent, whatever you need to do, but don't lock up that anger and frustration completely.

The only way to survive being a caregiver is to depersonalize it. Be an observer of the situation and give yourself permission to be safe. Don't let this journey define you or who you want to be. I know, easier said than done, but most of us, when faced with unfathomable challenges, go into fight or flight mode. Being someone who feels the need to be right, I often chose to fight. In retrospect, I know that was wrong. It was like a battle of the minds with an unarmed opponent. But we often choose to do what we have to do to get through that moment.

> ... *I want to emerge from this anger, fear, immense sadness and pain with my spirit bruised from the battle but still intact. When this is all over, I want to find "me" again. Help me, Lord, to survive this war and find a stronger, yet better me.*

To be honest, I struggled with anger and resentment. I gave up a really good job, my freedom, and the future that we had painstakingly planned. For me, I knew I needed to see a counselor. Talking it over with someone not involved was critical to my getting through such a difficult trial. I was able to vent, cry, feel validated and hear a voice of reason with some practical coping skills. I urge anyone else struggling with any difficult situation in life to seek help. It's a sign of courage, not weakness, to admit that you don't have all the skills or abilities needed to cope with the difficulties life throws your way.

CHAPTER **17**

Gaslighting

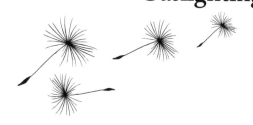

GASLIGHTING IS A TERM often used when someone is manipulating another person into questioning their own perception of reality, memory or mental stability. They make you feel like you're crazy or overreacting to a situation.

I never thought about this until our lives became embedded with dementia. Dan became so convinced in false truths that I started to doubt what I knew as factual reality. This was one major thing that could break my calmness like no other. I often found myself slipping back into fighter mode and arguing with him and trying to convince him why he was wrong. But he would also stand his ground and almost convince me that I was crazy and completely off base.

> *… I feel like I'm trying to have a battle of the minds with someone who is at a great disadvantage. You can't make sense out of nonsense. No matter how hard I try, it's an exercise in futility. I know that he can't connect the logical dots of facts with a brain incapable of even finding the dots. Why can't I just let it go? It's so hard, yet more*

effective, to just agree or walk away, yet I feel the need to convince him he's wrong. If I don't, I begin to question if I'm the one who has left reality.

It's hard to admit how much time and energy I wasted for many years trying to chase the reason he did something. I would question him and get an answer that made zero sense or was completely unrelated. For example, I would ask him why his toothbrush was on the bookshelf in the hallway. He would say because it's green. Then I would try to ask him again and that would lead to another nonsensical answer. Round and round this nondirectional conversation would go until I felt like I was the one losing my mind. That whole process accomplished nothing and left us both worn out, totally frustrated and angry.

... I feel like a slow learner. I find myself continually engaging in argumentative behavior. I know he's not gaslighting me. He doesn't have the conscious intent to do so. He believes what he believes. I really do try not to ask questions that I know will not produce an answer that I will understand, but sometimes my evil twin just can't help but ask that question to see what will come out of his mouth.

Sometimes I felt like I was trapped in an episode of *The Twilight Zone*. I became accustomed to his bizarre behavior day after day, then a family member would come over and the gaslighting began. During their brief visit, he would rise to the occasion and have moments of clarity and have the capacity for a normal conversation. That would give them validation that he's just fine and I must be stressing him out.

> … *Maybe I'm the one who's stressed out. Maybe I'm reading too much into his behavior. We all have off days. None of us are as sharp as we used to be. Maybe I should try CBD oil. Maybe we could both use it. I think I should start playing memory games on my phone instead of slot machines.*

The clear truth for those with dementia is that they have no malicious motives and therefore do not have the ability to gaslight. Although it can be so very difficult, especially in the earlier stages of the disease, it's best to meet them in their own reality. Yes, it can be so hurtful to you as a caregiver, but it is actually a show of respect to your loved one. In the end, it provides them with a safe and less anxious environment, which is a win for you as well!

CHAPTER **18**

Recharging

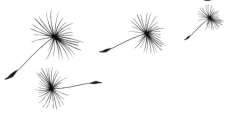

BEING A CAREGIVER OF SOMEONE YOU LOVE with dementia is a very long, arduous road. Day after day, you face monotonous and difficult circumstances. Month after month passes, then year after year, and you feel like you can't go on because you see no end in sight. Worse yet, you really don't want that end to come. I sometimes felt stuck in this downward spiral with little relief. It can sink your soul.

It's important to find ways to recharge and not only survive being a caregiver but to thrive. I tried to make a conscious effort to seek out and recognize the little joys and victories. Our time of quarantine during Covid made recharging especially difficult. I started a joy jar where I would write down at least one item per day that brought me a little sense of happiness or accomplishment. Some days, they were things like a card I received in the mail, an encouraging or funny phone call from a friend, dancing to a favorite song, watching a favorite movie, or getting a good night's rest. When I was feeling particularly blue and the pity party wanted to creep in, I'd take a peek at my joy jar and see the blessings adding up. Then I'd take a breath and know that joy was there if I chose to seek it out. On one especially rough day, I pulled out a slip of paper that said, "Today he smiled, winked at me, and called me pretty." Sigh…

We all have those days when we are full of self-doubt, guilt or coulda-woulda-shouldas. When one problem after another seemed to pile up and my limits were tested to the point of breaking, I tended not to show my warm and fuzzy side.

> … I have to remind myself that I'm human, and the last time I checked, no one is perfect. I'm really trying to do the best I can with the resolve I've been given. Even the most tepid water will boil over when it's heated enough. So, I lost it today. I know that chances are pretty good that he won't even remember it tomorrow, and therefore, certainly won't hold it against me. So why should I? I will do better tomorrow. I forgive myself today and will do something special for myself tomorrow. In the words of Aibileen Clark from the movie The Help: You is kind. You is smart. You is important.

One of the best ways to recharge is to practice self-care. No matter how well you think you may be doing, you can still use more. After some trying days, it would soon be a Joyce day, and I would get a break for a few hours. My favorite thing to do was read a book at the park and enjoy nature. On more than one of these occasions, the weather didn't cooperate and I sat in my car in a parking lot during a downpour. But I would put the seat back, turn on some music and savor every minute.

... Today was a recharge day for me. After Joyce arrived, I had an appointment to get the oil changed and tires rotated on my car. I know, how exciting. But I got to sit with others in the waiting room and have adult conversations. An employee asked if I would like a cup of hot chocolate on this blustery cold day, and I couldn't resist. She asked if I wanted marshmallows. Why not?! I felt quite regal and more relaxed than I have in many months, maybe years! I was actually disappointed when she came to tell me that my car was ready. But I left with a smile, feeling lighter and singing all the way home to, "The Lion Sleeps Tonight." And I think I will! Goodnight!

Of course I loved Dan deeply, but truth be told, some days I didn't like him. But my love kept me committed to care and provide for him. I found over the years that in order to do that sufficiently, I needed to care for myself, as well. Some days, I just needed to recharge and feel validated as a person, not just a caregiver. When a good friend recognized the depression I was beginning to feel, she told me to do some things just for me. She said to have an extra scoop of ice cream. Pour lots of hot fudge on top. Read the trashy novel. Find someone to relieve you. Go get your nails done. Have coffee with a friend. Treat yourself to your favorite restaurant.

... I love my spouse. I love my mom, kids, grandkids and friends. But I feel the need to love on myself, too. I'm not Atlas. The world does not rest on my shoulders. That's a myth I tell myself.

If I can give any caregiver one piece of advice, it's this: Be good to yourself. Take a break when you need one. It will help you come back to your loved one feeling more refreshed and ready to tackle challenges ahead. Open your heart to yourself. You are so worth it!

CHAPTER 19

A New Attitude

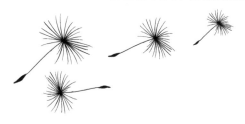

EVERY NEW YEAR'S DAY of each year that Dan was ill, I'd resolve to be more patient, more tolerable, more loving, and not allow those little irritants to get under my skin so easily.

> … I will not lose it when I answer the same question for the tenth time. I will not get angry when I clean up the mess or hunt for the lost item. I resolve to not judge when I see his socks on upside down with the heel on top or his shirt on backwards.
>
> Well that lasted until almost 2:00 in the afternoon. New record until I said, "Why are you peeing in the middle of the yard?! Were you born in a barn?! Get in here and get some clothes on. No, you can't go get the paper in your underwear."
>
> I'll try again next year to keep that resolution.

Weren't we always taught to enjoy the little things in life? The sunshine, gentle rain, a good night's sleep, the first flowers of spring peeking through, a warm chocolate chip cookie, toes in the sand, watching birds at a feeder, or a hot shower on a cool morning. In my experience of caring for Dan, it was the little things that built up and tested my patience. But it was also the little things that brought me joy. I just needed to adjust my attitude and recognize them as blessings. A rare thank you, a random smile, a touch on the cheek, or when he said, "You look nice today." The best was the occasional "I love you." Even though I'm apparently a slow learner, the worse he got, the more I was able to focus on a positive attitude, and those little things that used to drive me insane became less significant.

There were some days, however, that it would be incredibly hard to remain positive. After cleaning up messes of food, urine and feces, compounded with bizarre behavior and anger, the experts tell us to make it their best day ever. I suffered in silence, knowing that he was getting worse and I was losing myself along with him.

But if dementia has taught me anything, it's that I could never think too far into the future and worry about where I'll be or what I'll be. Dementia taught me that there is nothing more valuable than the present time. Tomorrow will be whatever it's meant to be. We have little choice as to how or when we die, but we can choose to make the most of today.

> *… I was thinking today about the word "brave." We, as caregivers, are often told that we are strong. Blah blah blah. Ok, we're strong. But today I'm thinking we're brave.*
>
> *We're brave to get up every morning, knowing that we're going to face new challenges and obstacles, and the old ones that didn't disappear overnight.*

*We're brave to keep putting one foot in front of the
other, even though we rarely get to go anywhere, while we
watch our family and friends run off to another party or
trip.*

*We're brave when we hide the tears that well up but
put our game faces on until we can safely cry in private.*

*We're brave because we often feel like giving up, but
we keep pressing on.*

I would often think back to my career days and imagine
what my job resume would look like after being a caregiver:

Investigative Specialist: All the time I spent gathering facts
and digging into what was wrong with my husband.

Research analyst: This goes hand in hand with the investiga-
tion. I dug into Google with all his symptoms and characteristics.
I researched tests and physicians that specialized in his condition.

Financial Expert: I learned to handle all the bills, insurance,
disability benefits, protecting our assets and planning for long-
term care.

Plant Operations Manager: This pretty much covers everything – cooking, cleaning, scheduling appointments, fixing the
garbage disposal, lawn maintenance, and cleaning up crap. In
general, I handled everything.

Chief Executive: No matter the task, big or small, I tackled
the project and plowed over barricades.

For me, the best change in attitude came from counseling.
What did I learn from these sessions? I learned to not sweat the
small stuff. Pick your battles. Count to 10. Don't always try to be
right. Wow, that last one was the toughest for me, but you will

never win an argument with someone who has dementia. I really did work on all of those things and it did help my attitude, which lowered Dan's overall anxiety.

I also found one peculiar thing that really helped. Show tunes. I love show tunes. So, when I found a dirty sock in the fridge, his slippers were on the wrong feet, or he peed in buckets in the garage, I belted out a chorus of "Let It Go! Let It Go!"

I waved my arms around while I sang, because it helped to really get into it. He may have stared at me like I was the one who lost it, and it didn't magically make everything right, but it de-escalated my rising frustration. Well, at least it worked sometimes. Sometimes, yes, because sometimes you just can't hold back any longer. Let it go! Let it go!

CHAPTER 20

Hope

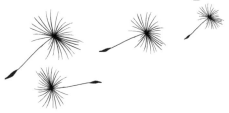

HOPE IS A FUNNY WORD. It's short, full of meaning and expectation. You desire a certain expectation. Before Dan was diagnosed, I kept alive that glimmer of hope that it was something else, something that a pill or special diet would cure or manage. Once we received his FTD diagnosis, I felt the loss of that hope. So, I then built my aspirations on it being a long, extended illness that could stay as normal as possible. However, as the years went by and it was clear that he was on a downward spiral, my meaning of hope changed once again.

> ... I like to think of the years before dementia as BD. The years after dementia as AD. During the BD era, conversations between us were so easy, simple, relaxed. Normal. How was your day? What do you think of that new recipe I tried? Can we afford to take a vacation?
>
> But in the AD era, I long for, I hope for days or even moments of such normal, easy conversations. I'm sorry I took the BD years for granted. They have been replaced with jumbled up words and sentences.

*But I like to think that I'm an eternally hopeful per-
son, so I will keep trying to find those moments of clarity. I
will keep hoping for those lucid times because it is getting
really tiring having conversations with myself. Talking to
myself is one thing, but I've started answering and even
arguing with myself.*

No matter how bad things got, how frustrated, confused and
lost he often was, there were some days with moments of clarity.
They may have been rare and fleeting, but they were the moments
I hoped for and cherished. I had hope that he was still in there and
we could hold on a little longer when I tucked him in at bedtime
and he smiled and said, "Thank you."

Three or four years into his illness, he would have really good
days, and I would try to convince myself that maybe, just maybe,
the diagnosis was wrong. It was a fluke or some other demon that
afflicted him had now left his body. But as the dementia progressed, I knew that these moments of clarity were simply neurons
that just happened to fire correctly instead of short-circuiting. I
learned over time to take full advantage of those moments. I knew
it would not last, and before long, the haze would roll back in and
confusion would take charge.

*… I often find myself losing hope. I feel like I work so hard
to provide care for him day after day, usually with little or
no gratitude or relief, knowing that the end result will still
be the same. No one gets out of this disease alive.*

*I find it so hard to feel hopeful for me as his care-
giver. Will there be a rainbow at the end of this storm?*

Daily, I feel the rain and the winds, and some days it's so hard to even imagine that there will be sunshine when this storm ceases.

I know that life will be different after the storm passes, but I must believe that there are thousands of wonderful experiences still waiting for me. So tomorrow I will don my raincoat, put on my galoshes, and weather the dark, threatening clouds and trudge through the storm. I have to believe in hope, and I have to focus on the rainbow ahead.

CHAPTER 21

Patient or Spouse?

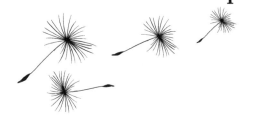

THERE COMES A MOMENT when you realize a switch has been flipped and you no longer feel like a spouse. You're a caregiver. Yes, in literal terms you're still a spouse, but emotionally, mentally, and physically, you've sidelined that status and are now a full-time caregiver. I was reminded of this when I was feeding him, bathing and shaving him, and cleaning up his incontinence. Thankfully, two things kept me going … my vows that we took many years ago and my deep, continued love.

Sometimes it's a gradual process, but for many, it's a sudden realization. For me, it was gradual. I tried to fight it. I tried to explain it away. I tried to make him the spouse I married until I gradually moved to another bedroom. His sleep patterns were so disruptive, and I knew that I needed, no craved, getting a good night's sleep. After all, the intimacy was long gone and sleep became so much more important.

> … If I am honest with myself, I look at my husband and see a stranger. When did he get replaced? The answer, of course, is not overnight. It was a gradual descent into the abyss of dementia.

I miss his face, his real face, not the mask he wears with FTD. I miss his ornery grin, the one that cared about me to the depth of his soul. The one that looked at me with such love and longing.

I look at him now and see a blank stare or eyes that don't focus. Or worse yet, I see a strange smile that will sometimes show up like that of a crazy person.

If I close my eyes, I can still conjure up memories of his real face, the one that made me smile and assured me that everything would be ok. God, let me never forget that face.

One of the hardest things for me as a caregiver was having to make all the decisions, and I mean ALL the decisions. As a spouse, we had those things we were each good at and those issues that we discussed and decided on together. If something around the house needed repaired, it was all on him. Most things he could fix and, if not, he hired someone. He would make the calls, get the bids, discuss the project and coordinate it all. Then I paid the bills after completion. Now it's all up to me. I learned to fix a leaky faucet, a plugged drain, put new string on the weed whacker, and change the filter in the furnace. I've coordinated the projects to replace doors, install a new driveway, put on a new roof and replace our kitchen countertops.

Taking over all of this didn't mean that he didn't TRY to get involved. I remember the day I had a salesman at our house to order new front and rear doors. Dan kept insisting that he look at our gutters. He was not a gutter salesman. The patience of that poor man was commendable. I had forewarned him about Dan's dementia, and now he listened to him intently. He even went outside and climbed up on a ladder and looked at the gutters. He just gave me a wink that silently said, "It's ok. I got this." I found myself truly believing in the goodness of humankind that day.

But, if I were to be completely honest, I often felt that being the caregiver of a husband with dementia is like having an anchor tied around my spirit. Try as I might, it was so hard to elevate and maintain a positive attitude and outlet. I felt like my life was slowly swirling down the drain, while the lives around me kept propelling forward.

> *... Stuck. That's the key word for how I feel. I miss the future, the one that we had planned, the reason we've worked, scrimped and saved. I even miss the impulsive fun we used to have. With dementia, impulsive isn't really in the vocabulary. We can't just jump in the car and take off for a fun adventure. There's too much planning and necessary preparing. It's even hard to go get groceries!*
>
> *Stuck. Not only are our planned futures gone but we can't make new plans because we don't know when that will be or what that will look like.*
>
> *But I know there will be a future. Dare I set goals and dream?*

I often felt envious of those caregivers who say how much they love their spouse, feel so privileged to be taking care of them, and love them more each day. I guess that's what we would all want, but I often wasn't in that frame of mind. Yes, I loved my husband. Still do. It's that love and commitment that kept me going through the nightmare. But after years of being his caregiver, it felt more like the love of a soul mate and not a marital partner.

> *… Years of emotional distancing have left me somewhat calloused and often feeling uncomfortable with him. It's so strange to feel so alone with him right there beside me. I feel so disconnected when we're in the car, watching TV and eating dinner.*
>
> *I'll always be here for him. I'll help him, advocate for him and strive to keep him fed, clean and as healthy as possible. I'll always love him, but the spark is gone, which makes me feel so sad and lonely. I miss our intimacy, feeling loved, and having that partner who makes me feel special and wanted.*

When you love someone with dementia, they can try the very fiber of your presence. They often don't reciprocate your love as the disease progresses. There were times when his words were inexplicably hurtful, even after giving my all to him. Even though they were words from a damaged brain, infested by dementia, they still hurt. When his words cut like a knife, I tried to put a band-aid on my hurt feelings, but it was so very difficult. I tried to remind myself that he was acting out of fear, and I was his safe place to express his frustration and anger. He knew that I would love him in spite of the bruises he left on my heart.

Yes, there were moments of sunshine when his face lit up when he saw me. I know that his love was apparent when he showed his dependence on me. He felt safe to get angry at me because he knew I wouldn't leave him. There were also times that we would both end up in laughter while trying to get him dressed, especially one day when he started without me and tried to dress himself. He had gotten into my dresser drawer instead of his own and was holding up a girdle-type garment trying to figure out how it went on. We both laughed until we cried.

Probably the hardest part about losing your spouse while they're still here physically but not mentally is that you don't have that partner to share those emotional highs and lows. The event that affected me the most was when my only brother, John, died of ALS at age 66. It was sudden and unexpected. He had been diagnosed only eight months prior, although he had been struggling for quite a while before they figured out what was happening. On Christmas Eve morning, 2021, John suddenly collapsed in his bathroom. They feel he either aspirated or his diaphragm just gave out and he couldn't breathe.

The grief was overwhelming and consuming. I was trying to care for Dan, console my then 94-year-old mom over the loss of her only son, as well as my brother's family, and at the same time deal with my own grief and awareness that my husband most likely would be next.

Dan's dementia was advanced enough at that point that he couldn't attend any services, and I felt so alone, craving my once strong, caring husband's arms to hold and comfort me. When the services and luncheon were over, I arrived home to an exhausted caregiver who was helping us out and a husband who wanted to know where I'd been and what was for dinner.

It can be gut wrenching to keep giving when receiving little to nothing in return. I felt more at peace with loving him when I learned to accept him for where he was in the current moment. I had to keep reminding myself that he didn't choose his behavior. It certainly wasn't easy to reach that level of acceptance, and I often failed. But when I succeeded, it was worth the effort and helped both of us obtain calmness and healing.

CHAPTER 22

Where Did I Go?

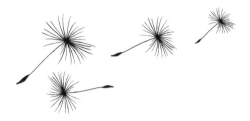

SOMEONE ONCE SAID TO ME, "Your husband is really declining." I answered, "Yes, he is." What I didn't say is that I was declining, too.

> ... *I have felt so very alone for so long, and yet, I'm not alone. He sits there beside me every day. We have nonsensical conversations, and I've all but ceased trying to make sense out of nonsense.*

I learned shortcuts to adapt to new losses and challenges. I gave up things in our home that used to be so important, like order and cleanliness. I learned to pick my battles. With each new adaption, each relinquishment of important tasks, social connections or self-indulgences, I lost a little more of "me" and wondered how much of it would ever return.

I have a strong faith, and that faith is what got me through some pretty rough days. People often asked how God can allow things like cancer or dementia to happen, and how I could remain strong in my faith through so many years of losses. I feel that God gives us free will and helps us to push through these trials so that we can learn and grow from them. I know that I learned I'm a lot stronger than I ever imagined I could be, even though I still hate that word "strong." I've learned to be more patient and kind.

But I also know that I was physically and emotionally tired. I often wondered if I was just a slow learner or if I hadn't suffered enough yet. Which was it, God? There were days when nothing, absolutely nothing seemed to go right. I had cleaned up one mess after another, heard or read about the great time my friends had on their trips, and I turned down yet another invitation to lunch. I felt more alone than ever.

> *... This day is finally done. I lie here in bed hoping that I'll fall asleep before I fall apart. God, please remind me that I matter. I made such an effort today to make his favorite foods, put his favorite shows on TV, and remind him that I love him. I was met with frustration, anger, and cleaning up pee out of the living room carpet. Please, God, remind me that I matter, too. I feel like without me, so many things would fall apart – the house, the bills, his meds and appointments. You've made me a talented juggler, but I need to know that I matter and am loved.*

I've always thought that Post Traumatic Stress Disorder (PTSD) was something that was only experienced by survivors of great trauma like war, sexual assault or domestic violence. However, I realized that the longer I was a dementia caregiver, I thought that I had PTSD. The emotional toll on me taking care of Dan was tremendous. It had left me with flashbacks, anxiety, guilt, depression and significant mood swings, which are all signs of PTSD.

In retrospect, I wish I could have had the insight to give myself a big batch of grace at the end of every day. I had more than my share of losses, hard decisions and grief. I wish I could have focused more on what went right and what I did right.

Going through hard times leaves us with a lasting impression. It alters us and changes the way we view so many things. We may be more sympathetic, kind and patient. There are undoubtedly empty spaces in my life where people who were important to us have left, but new things will and do grow in those spaces. You just have to be open to them.

PART THREE

The Final Chapter

CHAPTER 23

End of Care Choices

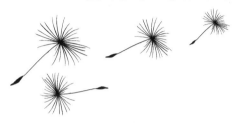

No one chooses to suffer from dementia or to be that person caring for a loved one with this illness. Given the option, we'd all get off the train at the next depot. To be honest, I probably wouldn't even wait for it to stop. I'd just look for my opportunity at the next curve and do a jump, tuck and roll.

Everyone on this path has different life circumstances, and we all travel with different baggage. There are some with young children at home, some have parents they are caring for, and some are in that sandwich generation with both. God help them! Some, like me, are home alone with their loved one, feeling very lonely, but not alone.

Many people are able to care for their loved one until the end, while others must work or just can't physically or mentally provide the care required. Whatever the circumstances, the road is hard and life-changing. It's a personal decision as to whether or not you choose to keep your loved one at home, and it's important to support the caregiver in whatever decision is made.

Believe me, I weighed the decision to place Dan in memory care for a long time, years, and it was the hardest decision of our entire journey. He had always asked me to keep him home as long as possible, and I certainly wanted to meet his wishes. As he became much worse, my family and friends urged me to place him. I prayed hard about the decision, probably the entire last year he was at home. His decline was getting much more difficult on both of us, to the point that I felt I was losing myself along with him.

> *... I've always been told, "You'll know when it's time." Will I? There are days when I think that is true, but there are also other days when I think that I'm going to phys- ically or mentally wear out before I make that decision.*
>
> *Some say, "You'll know when you're done." Well, will I know when I'm done? Will it be possible to keep a little of myself for me? I fear not having any life left over when that final chapter comes because I am so worn out from being and doing everything for so long.*

We were into the tenth year of his illness when his decline really started to escalate. I had been totally dressing him for the last year and a half, and now I was helping him shower, along with cleaning up the incontinence episodes that were increasing. He started getting up multiple times during the night to use the bath- room, but would be confused and not be able to find it. There were accidents in his bedroom, my bedroom, the living room floor and even the kitchen.

Then the falls and mini seizures and strokes started to occur. He was 6'1" and I'm 5'6" with a bad back and not even a year out since my major spine surgery. I struggled to get him up, and began to fear that he was going to fall and break something – or me. We had one incident of a mini stroke occurring when Kelly was there. He even stopped breathing for a bit. We called 911 and he was taken to the hospital, checked out, and released. But it caused additional fear and concern for all of us, not knowing what scary issue would be next.

I knew that I needed some relief. He was not keen on having home health come in, so we discussed another option. The memory care facility near us had just re-opened their adult day care services after having been closed for two years from the Covid epidemic. I got him enrolled and he started going there on Mondays and Fridays from 11:00 – 3:00, and our angel, Joyce, still came on Wednesday afternoons. This gave me four hours of respite on three days each to take care of errands, have lunch with a friend, or spend time with my mom.

My real "aha" moment came on March 23, 2022. He was having a particularly bad day with much confusion and unsteadiness. The night before, he fell trying to get out of bed to go to the bathroom and was wedged between the bed and the wall, hurting his back. Somehow, I managed to get him to the bathroom and back to bed. Then in the morning, I was in our garage getting the trash ready for pickup when he came out trying to "help" me. As he suddenly started staggering backwards, I grabbed hold of him and eased him back into the utility room. My intent was to get him back in his recliner. But as he tried to manage the two steps up into our kitchen, he started to fall. I couldn't stop him, and he came down hard, with half of his body lying in the kitchen and half across the steps. I tried repeatedly to get him up, but he had no strength, and I didn't have enough.

After several attempts, I finally got him to half crawl, with me pulling him through the kitchen, into the living room, and finally into his recliner. I knew that there was no way I was going to get him back up to do anything! I sent a text to the girls that we were in trouble and Becky was able to leave work to come help me.

In the meantime, I called his family doctor and was instructed to either call 911 or take him to the emergency room ourselves. So, I waited for Becky, who came within 15 minutes. We planned to take him to the hospital, but, of course, he wanted to go to the bathroom first. We literally dragged him to the toilet, sat him down, and then dragged him to the car. I still don't know how we accomplished that feat!

At the hospital, he had bloodwork, a chest x-ray, a CT scan of his head and a urinalysis. The latter was quite the chore to get. We tried a bedside urinal, standing him up, coaxing and pleading. He refused until we got him to the restroom. Even though all of the tests came back ok, they presumed he had another mini stroke and was admitted for observation.

At this point, both girls took me aside and said, "It's time, Mom. You've done a great job taking care of him at home, but it's not safe for either of you anymore."

That was the aha moment when I knew what I had to do.

Social services became involved, and a plan was put into action. He would stay for the next couple of days in the hospital, then go into a skilled facility for about a week and get some therapy to improve his strength and walking. After that period, he would be placed permanently into the memory care center. That first night that I went home, alone, was one of the hardest moments ever. I walked into an empty house with his things still visible here and there. I knew in my heart that he would never return.

> ... *The house is too quiet. I kneel on the floor next to his empty bed and cry like I've never cried before. I don't even recognize the anguished loud sobs coming from me. He's gone. He's gone from our home. Not just mentally this time, but physically, too.*
>
> *I've been losing him for so long. I've been saying goodbye for so long. Everything about him has been dying for so long, except him – our dreams, our goals, our future, our friendships, his independence.*
>
> *This is the end of a big chapter in our marriage. He's not coming back here. Even though I kept my promise of keeping him at home for as long as I possibly could, I still feel guilty.*

CHAPTER 24

Adjusting to Placement

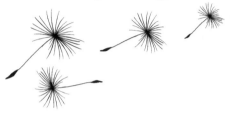

A FEW DAYS AFTER DAN HAD BEEN IN SKILLED CARE, it was time to move him to his new home in the memory care wing of the same facility. Luckily, he was placed in the same room he had been using for the adult respite care days, so there was a level of comfort and familiarity for him. My 72-year-old sister happened to be in the same memory care center, suffering from Alzheimer's. So, I was able to visit both of them each day. We brought some items from home to make Dan more comfortable – his favorite recliner, his favorite throw blanket and some family pictures.

As the facility was only 10 minutes away, I went to see him every day and stayed about an hour and a half, usually around lunchtime. He had started having increased vision deficits, which made eating even more difficult. Being there at lunchtime allowed me to help him eat and make sure that he was getting enough nutrition.

> ... I requested that they serve him finger foods because he doesn't have enough executive function anymore to use utensils. I noticed that every single day at lunch they brought him

chicken tenders and French fries. He never complained, but I thought it was ridiculous that they couldn't find something else. I finally spoke up today and asked, "Don't you have anything else?" They said that I had requested finger foods. I told them most things could be adjusted. A hamburger or chicken could be cut up. He could pick up green beans and other vegetables with his fingers. They looked at me like I was being completely unreasonable.

We gradually grew into a routine. After I fed him lunch, we would go to his room and visit in private. I bought one of those digital frames with a big screen and encouraged family members to send pictures. When I pulled him up close, he enjoyed seeing the kids, grandkids, and even his siblings. Eventually, his vision became so bad that he struggled to make out the people. As the doctor explained it, his eyes weren't getting worse, but his occipital lobe had shrunk to the point that his brain couldn't process the images coming in. This was all part of his Posterior Cortical Atrophy, another form of dementia. When he reached for things, he was always off a bit because his depth perception was gravely impaired, which frustrated him and increased his anxiety.

Eventually, I became more accustomed to living alone. A few months after he was placed in memory care, I began the arduous task of cleaning out drawers and cupboards that were "his." He once had been such a compulsive, organized man, but the disarray now seemed to mirror what was going on in his brain.

… Tucked away, I found a new, unused Valentine's Day card today, complete with an envelope. It read, "For My

Wife" and hadn't been signed yet. Apparently, it was at least six or seven years old when he was still able to drive. Seeing it brought on a watershed moment and the sweet remembrance of how much he loved me.

Going through these things are tugging at my heart, but I know there's a purpose for my pain and tears. They are tangible reminders of the good times and the life we lived together.

All in all, I knew the decision to place him was the right one, even if the guilt monster still visited me from time to time. I think that's normal. You always wonder about the "what ifs." But I started making plans with friends and visiting him daily. I even got to be a Mom and Grandma again, attending family gatherings and going to sporting events. I got to cheer for them in live time and not just hear about it after the fact.

… Although I had been sacrificing everything to keep him at home, I find that I'm starting to feel like his wife again. I am his spouse and not an exhausted caregiver. I can give him the best of me while I'm there each day. I feel my love for him increasing. I look forward to our visits and he looks forward to my arrival. Giving up his caregiving to the professionals was the right thing to do. I feel a closeness to him that I haven't felt in a long time. I am his advocate. I am his wife.

We were able to have some very good days while he was in the memory care center. I often walked him out to the patio and

I would play our beloved oldies songs. He would smile and sway and tell me he loved me. My girls and his siblings came to visit as well as a few friends. His buddy, Joyce, would stop periodically to visit and they would still share a laugh and an ornery conversation.

Once I could return to being Grandma, I was able take care of the little grandsons now and then. On one particular day, I brought our youngest grandson to visit. He watched me punch in the code to the memory center, we had a nice visit with grandpa, and he watched me punch in the code to get back out. On the walk to my car, his little 5-year-old brain was turning and he looked up at me and asked, "Why is Pawpaw locked up?"

When I told him that his brain was sick, he said, "I know that. But why is he locked up?" I told him that we didn't want him to go anywhere that he would hurt himself. He said, "Oh! I get it. But is it jail?" I said, "No, it's not jail."

A few hours later, I took him to my granddaughter's track meet and his Aunt Kelly, who was standing about 30 feet away, shouted out to him, "Sebastian, did you see Pawpaw today?" He shouted back, "Ya, he's locked up, but he's not in jail!" Everyone laughed, and life seemed almost normal again.

CHAPTER 25

The Beginning of the End

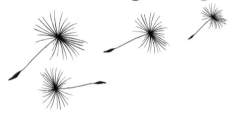

IF I HAD ONLY KNOWN that things weren't just going from bad to worse, but THE worst. I really didn't see this coming. Yes, he was steadily declining, but I had no idea we were now skiing down the mountain at warp speed and hitting every obstacle on the way.

> *... Dan seems to be fading away more each day now. I feel like it's too late to say goodbye. He smiles when I visit, but there's this vacant look in his eyes. He has started hallucinating and talks about little kids in the corner of his room. I don't argue. I don't even speak. I just want to scream.*

He seemed to be having more difficulty walking, more frequent incontinent moments, and his vision was diminishing. His anxiety attacks were becoming more prominent, and the medications to control them didn't seem to be helping. I began getting calls from the staff saying that they couldn't get him settled and asking if I could come try to calm him down. I would always pull up a chair beside him in his recliner so that I could stroke his arm, rub his temples and talk to him about the kids and grandkids.

These simple gestures of love would always relax him, but he began to say that he was ready to go. I knew what he meant. He was ready to go see Jesus.

Palliative care workers came a few days later and met with Becky and me. We answered a lot of questions and then they met with Dan and studied his current physical and mental condition. The conclusion of that visit was that he qualified for hospice. I was shocked and so unprepared to hear that word. I saw their visit resulting in changes in medication to help with his anxiety and making him more comfortable. But they saw it differently. His rapid weight decline, difficulty walking, vision loss, and inability to obtain or recognize comfortable body temperatures were all signs that things were progressing. We agreed to place him on hospice, having no idea what was about to happen.

Four days later, the hospice nurse and social worker arrived. There were a lot of questions and a lot of uncomfortable discussions, but there was also this reassurance that they were there to help. It was a relief knowing that there was a team of caregivers who were saying, "We're here to take this burden off of your shoulders. As we care for him, we will also be caring for you and your family."

Although it was sad that we were at this point, I felt my shoulders relax and didn't feel that weight of caregiving that I had experienced for the past 10 years. After the nurse and social worker examined Dan and talked with him, they felt he still had months. We even discussed the possibility of taking him off hospice, if he plateaued.

Medication changes were ordered in an effort to reduce his anxiety, promote better sleep, and reduce his depression. For a couple of days, we settled back into the routine of visits at lunchtime and enjoying cuddles and golden oldie tunes. But the tide was about to change …

Five days after signing his admission into hospice, I arrived at the care center and ran into another patient's family member exiting. She said, "Dan isn't feeling well. He stopped me and said something was wrong with him."

I thanked her and punched in the code for the memory unity. As soon as I got near his room, I felt the change. He was standing in the middle of his room with a sheer panic expression on his face. I asked him, "What's wrong, honey?"

He replied, "Where's Mary? I need Mary!"

I said, "I'm here, honey. It's me, Mary."

He yelled, "I need my Mary!" I grabbed him by both shoulders, and said, "It's me. It's your Mary. What's going on?"

He said, "Something's wrong with me."

I coaxed him to sit in his recliner, trying to assure him all the while that everything was ok. I pulled up a chair beside him, held his arm, his hand, stroked his face and kept reminding him that I was there. His Mary was there. I stayed extra long that day. He ate well, I helped him to the bathroom, and tried to squelch the panic I felt rising in my gut.

I was able to get him relaxed enough after lunch to lie down for a nap, but his eyes were wild and wide open. So, I sat with him, rubbed his back and sang softly to him. As I felt his muscles relax, his eyes began to flutter and I was able to get him to close his eyes. I tiptoed out of the room, drove home with the tears free falling down that mountain of strength that everybody kept telling me I possessed. I believe today that he knew the avalanche was coming.

He sensed it. I knew there was something different, something inescapably scary and sad coming. I just didn't know how soon. As I lay in bed that night, begging sleep, I caught myself holding my breath several times. I willed myself to breathe. Tomorrow will be a new day. That's it. It was probably just a bad day.

The next morning, I woke up with great promise. It was Sunday. The sun was shining and I had had a good night's rest. I went through the usual motions of a bowl of cereal and a hot cup of coffee. I enjoyed some sewing and planned my day around my lunch with him. Then the phone rang at 10:30, an hour before my normal visitation time. It was the care center. The nurse said that they were really struggling with Dan. He was yelling, even throwing things, and they couldn't settle him down. He kept saying he needed Mary. I told them I'd be there in a few minutes. When I left the house, I had no idea that our lives would forever change from that moment forward.

When I walked into his room, it was a carbon copy of the prior day. He was standing in the middle of his room, screaming my name. I kept telling him that I was there.

"Dan, it's me. Your Mary."

I got him to sit in his chair and when I repeated the calming mantra and sang an old song we loved, I could feel him begin to relax.

Soon it was lunchtime, and I asked that they bring it into his room. I wasn't going to upset the peace by trying to walk him to the dining area. After trying to feed him a few bites, I realized that he wasn't swallowing anything. It was all pocketed inside his cheek. So, I coaxed and was able to get him to swallow it. But I had to remind him after each bite. It became more of a battle, and after eating only about a fourth of his food, he refused any more and said he was tired.

I helped him get into bed, and as soon as I got him comfortable, he wanted to use the bathroom. I tried to get him up, but it was as if his legs wouldn't work. I called for help and with assistance from the nurse and an aide, we got him to the toilet. He couldn't go. We let him sit there a bit and then got him back in bed. Two minutes later, it was a repeat.

He became more and more agitated and uncontrollable. Hospice was called and I texted both of the girls that there was a huge change. Kelly responded that she was on her way. Becky was on her way home from Columbus. After Kelly arrived, we were literally holding him down. Tears were pouring from our eyes and I asked the nurse, "What's next?"

We couldn't keep physically holding him down forever. What could be done? The answer was morphine. I knew what that meant. It was the beginning of the end.

CHAPTER 26

Dying Is a Process

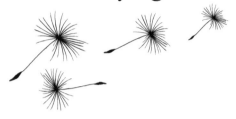

THE NEXT FEW HOURS were a blur of trying multiple medications to calm him as much as possible. During that time, we were asked to leave the room, while they held him down to place a catheter. Eventually, the med cocktail took effect and there was stillness, except for occasional twitches in his legs and arms.

I decided it was time to let his siblings and my family members know that there had been this significant change. It was time to let loved ones know that he was dying. Becky arrived and we sat vigil the rest of the day together, not knowing what to expect. The staff kept him pretty much sedated. Our girls went home late that evening and I stayed in the recliner at his bedside, trying to sleep off and on.

When morning came, the girls were back and there was no major change. All of his siblings (Dan was one of nine) showed up that morning and the facility put up with the crowd. He would have hated all that noise, but it wasn't about him at that point. This was their opportunity to say goodbye to their brother, reminisce and find comfort in their memories. A couple of them brought back lunch for everyone, and they stayed until late afternoon. Most of them left, knowing that would be the last time they would see him.

The girls and I fell into a routine of staying by his side throughout the day. I would go home in the evening and sleep for a couple of hours and then relieve them, so that they could go home and sleep through the night. At one point, the priest came in and gave him last rites and the apostolic blessing.

His body went through so many changes due to organ failure, but his heart kept on ticking strong. They suspected he was having strokes, as his mouth was drooping and at one point, his left leg went completely white and had no pulse. The next day it had pinked back up and had a pulse. This went on for four days.

On the last evening, I had gone home around 8:00 and told the girls I'd be back at 11:00. I showered and tried to sleep but I had this gnawing feeling that he was leaving. I ended up being back by 9:30 and saw that his breathing was more rapid and he was gurgling. The girls went home and I spent that night by his side, listening to his every breath. Since sleep would not come, I spent much of my time writing his obituary. It didn't feel strange or faze me.

When the sun came up, his breathing was even more rapid and his legs were starting to mottle, a sure sign that he was transitioning. I put my head on his chest and sang the song he loved so well: *I think we're alone now, the beating of my heart is the only sound...*

Becky got there around 9:00 and after I told her that he was leaving us soon, she texted Kelly, who quickly made arrangements for someone to cover her classroom. His vital signs indicated impending death, which the hospice nurse confirmed. I sat and prayed and said goodbye over and over and over. I reminded him of his promise to give me a sign after he went to heaven that he was ok.

Suddenly, his last gasps came. When I saw Kelly pulling into the parking lot, I told him to hang on two more minutes, so that she could say goodbye. As she ran into the room, he took his last final breath and was gone.

Ten years. Ten years brought us to this heart-wrenching moment. Damn that FTD. But I was grateful it was over. After the endless grieving and watching him slowly leave us, the final ultimate loss had come. Our beloved husband, father, grandfather, brother and friend was gone. He was now whole again with no more dementia and no more suffering. God called him home.

Epilogue

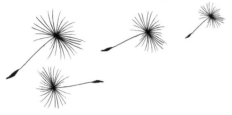

WHEN YOU HAVE BEEN WITH SOMEONE FOR 45 YEARS, they become a part of you. I didn't know who I was or would be without Dan in my life. While driving home from the memory care center right after his death, it hit me that I was now a widow.

> *… It's difficult to describe how I feel. Dan is finally free. I waited for this day and even prayed for it. He was miserable and has been ready to go home. I don't regret my time with him, not even the moments that were filled with hurt and sorrow. In the end, it's not what I've been through, but how I got through it that has made me the person I am today, and the person who I am capable of being tomorrow. But who is that?*

A month or so before he died, we had a really meaningful heart-to-heart conversation. I told him how much I loved him, and when he was ready, to just let go and ask God to take him home. He said he was ready and loved me, too. It was the first time, in a long time, he had said that.

About a week after he passed, I was sitting in my recliner with my coffee, having a bit of a pity party. I said out loud, "Honey, it's been a week and I haven't gotten a sign from you yet." I sat very still for a few seconds and felt nothing. The tears started coming. Then I heard a noise in the kitchen and couldn't figure out what it was. When I walked in to investigate, I saw a piece of paper that was starting to spit out of the printer. I picked it up and there it was. Daniel J. Verhoff was typed at the top of the page and nothing else on it. I hadn't been at that printer in over a week. I looked up and said, "Thank you, honey. Thank you, God!" Then I bawled my eyes out.

The next day, I sat down in the recliner with my morning coffee and thanked him again for the sign. I went into the kitchen to grab a granola bar, and when I returned, there was a small white piece of paper lying on the middle of the seat. It hadn't been there before. I picked it up, turned it over, and saw a photo of Dan, dressed as a clown, riding a lawn tractor in our town's bicentennial parade back in 1976. I smiled, cried, and thanked him again.

There were several more subtle signs, and God-wink moments that followed, assuring me that he is whole again and catching the big ones in paradise.

> ... *Dear Journal, I think it's time to say goodbye, for now. You have been my anchor through this storm. The dandelion seeds have all blown away, but I see new growth on the horizon. I'm trying to have more good days than bad, but grief is a process. It's the price we pay for love. I still have "sloth" days when I can't seem to put one foot in front of the other. When that happens, I lock the door and allow myself to grieve and try to remember Dan in his BD days.*

Once I finished all of the post-death tasks, things were finalized about eight months later. I made a promise to myself to make deliberate choices and decisions that would bring me joy and peace. If that meant putting on my pajamas at 7:00 p.m., then so be it. If it meant a day trip with a friend to a winery, great. If it meant curling up with a good book, ok. If it meant letting go of relationships that were toxic and self-serving, so much the better. I'm not ready for big trips or any major life decisions just yet, and continue to try to fill my life with small joys.

It took me a few weeks to get up the courage to go visit my sister in the memory care center. When I did, there were a lot of tears that first time. I still get a strange unsettling feeling when I walk past the room where Dan had been. But now my 96-year-old mom is in assisted living in the same facility, so I'm again visiting two loved ones, albeit in different units.

About 18 months after his death, one of my favorite healing moments happened. Kelly came to pick something up and said, "Mom, I'm going to tell you something, and it will probably make you cry. I am so proud of you. You took such good care of Dad for such a long time. Now you're taking care of Grandma, visiting Aunt Carol, going out with friends, playing dominoes, and doing things that bring you joy. I'm just so very proud of you."

And yes, I cried. Happy tears and sad tears. Tears of grief and tears of joy. Tears that were letting go of so many years of feeling guilty for not being enough. In Kelly's eyes, I was enough and more.

Yes, there are still tears, almost daily, but I'm learning to live with the grief and still move forward. The last thing Dan would want is for me to wallow in self-pity. I think if I were to do that, he'd send me a big sign that he was going to kick my butt. I will always love him. That doesn't disappear after 45 years of marriage, even after the difficult journey we endured. So, until I see him again, I will continue to seek out joy and Just Breathe.

Acknowledgments

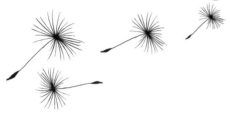

THIS BOOK could not have been written without the love and confidence that my husband, Dan, instilled in me for over 45 years. I dedicate our story to him, who showed much strength and dignity throughout his illness.

I am grateful to our daughters, Kelly and Becky, for helping me push through those bad days, remembering the good ones, and showering us with love and laughter.

Thank you to my mom, Julie Koch, for always providing emotional support. The wisdom of her 96 years and having been a widow for the last 35 of those, gave me great insight from someone who truly understands grief and loss.

Because of special friends, especially Joyce Wiley, I was able to recharge and endure some pretty dark days.

A special thank you goes to Jodie L. (Bunn) Niese for her photographic talent and giving me the perfect image for the cover.

Last but not least, I offer endless gratitude to Beth Huffman for her encouragement and helping me structure our journey into a richer and more poignant story. Beth is simply amazing.

If you have questions or comments, feel free to email me at: dverhoff1@woh.rr.com.

Printed in the USA
CPSIA information can be obtained
at www.ICGtesting.com
LVHW021916060924
790241LV00040B/935